FIRST S

The handbook to 1

Stephen Gaukroger

WIPF & STOCK · Eugene, Oregon

Wipf and Stock Publishers
199 W 8th Ave, Suite 3
Eugene, OR 97401

First Steps
The Handbook to Following Christ
By Gaukroger, Stephen
Copyright©2019 Apostolos
ISBN 13: 978-1-5326-9600-8
Publication date 7/7/2019
Previously published by Apostolos, 2019

Illustrations by Rowin Agarao

FIRST STEPS
The handbook to following Christ

Stephen Gaukroger

To the elders and staff at Gold Hill

Contents

About the author

Stephen Gaukroger, born in Sheffield, was converted, baptized and called to the pastoral ministry while attending Carey Baptist church in Preston, Lancashire. Following training at Spurgeon's College, he spent a year on the staff of First Baptist Church, Dallas, Texas.

Currently, he is Senior Minister at Gold Hill Baptist Church, one of the largest Baptist churches in England. He is a prolific author with a popular style. Many of his 19 books have been widely translated.

Stephen is regarded as one of the most significant leaders of his generation in the UK. He has a clear grasp of postmodern culture and addresses its challenges with an unquestioned commitment to Scripture.

He regards mission/evangelism as a key priority for the church, both locally and nationally, and it is this reality which drives his leadership. Stephen has been influential in the leadership of Spring Harvest, widely recognized as the most significant Christian teaching event of the last 25 years, and he remains a member of the Spring Harvest Council. He was President of the Baptist Union of Great Britain from 1994–5, and now serves on the Council of Spurgeon's College, and also chairs the Council of Reference of the European branch of Jews for Jesus.

He is married to Janet, who is very involved with Christian work among under 5s and worship, and they have three children.

How to get the best out of FIRST STEPS

This book will help you take your first steps as a Christian. It will help you lay the foundations for a strong Christian life. It will point to some of the possibilities now open to you. Approach each new chapter prayerfully, read it carefully, and think about whether the material prompts you to consider taking any action.

One of the most useful ways of reading this book is to make it a group experience! Perhaps your church has a range of small groups and one or more of those may be composed of newcomers to the faith like yourself. Or you may want to create an informal group – which could be as small as you and two others – with friends or contacts you know who, like you, want to know more about following Christ. Reading this book, chapter by chapter, and sharing your thoughts and responses together in a discussion can be really rewarding.

Being in a small group like this has a number of real advantages. You may feel that by becoming a Christian you have distanced yourself from some of your existing support and friendship structures and so feel a bit out on a limb. In a small group, you will find a fresh source of support and encouragement.

Perhaps you have lots of questions about your newfound faith. The small group is a great place to share those! You may find some answers; certainly, you will discover that you are not alone in your doubts.

Perhaps you are struggling with the experience of fitting into the church. Then the small group will certainly help in that uncomfortable transition period. Or you might be wondering what you have to offer to the church or to God. Within a small group, you will be able to explore the gifting God has most certainly given you, and you will discover something of the plans that God has for you in the wider church family.

If it's a matter of setting up a small group from scratch, all you need to do is to find a place where you can meet undisturbed for an hour or an hour and a half each week. Do let your church leader know your plans so that he can pray for you as a group, be available if you need any help and possibly link you up with others who would benefit from the group.

Each person in the group needs to have a copy of this book and a Bible. Everyone agrees together to read a chapter of First Steps each week before the meeting. At the end of each chapter, you will find some questions and activities which you can use as a framework for your group discussion.

For some sessions, a little preparation will be needed. Sometimes, for example, it will be useful to have a supply of pens and paper handy. For session three, it could be very meaningful to share bread and wine together – but this will need a little advance thinking and planning by one of the group. In session six you'll need to get hold of three or four different versions of the Bible to look at and, if possible, any commentaries you can borrow on 2 Timothy.

Enjoy!

Stephen Gaukroger

1

Starting out

So you've become a Christian. Fantastic! It's the most important commitment you could ever have made.

The potential for every new Christian is incredible. I'm pretty sure that at the moment you have only the merest glimmer of what could be in store for you. Every wrong thing you have ever done has been forgiven. You have become a new person, a child of God with a wonderful heavenly Father. For you, death is not the end of everything because you have been given God's cast iron guarantee of life with him forever. Your eternal future is absolutely secure.

There are many other things to benefit you, too. Like a new family to love and support you. Then there's the special power God has given you in your life to defeat wrong and help others. Add to that the different kinds of gifts God wants you to have. The list goes on ...

It sounds too good to be true – but it's not! However, it's sadly true that many Christians do not experience all these things in the way God wants them to. But they are available, even if some do not take advantage of them.

You are at the beginning of a journey. Sometimes it will be a difficult uphill climb. Sometimes you will feel you are making no progress at all, and you may feel like giving up. Thankfully, the journey will not be without its encouragements. Often the clouds will lift to reveal breath-taking scenery. There will be times of certainty that you are on the right road. Your experiences along the way will often spur you on to greater heights. At the summit, you will discover a new view too marvelous to be described in words!

Facts and feelings

You may be reeling from the excitement of your new commitment. Or you may just not feel any different at all from the way you did before deciding to follow Christ. Are you on cloud nine or under cloud one? Whatever your feelings, it will help you to establish the facts about what has happened to you.

And facts they most certainly are. It is a fact of history that Jesus Christ lived and died. That he was raised from the dead is supported by substantial evidence and no one has been able to disprove it, despite many and continuing attempts to do so.

Despite popular opinion, the Bible is not riddled with contradictions or errors. It is a thoroughly reliable document, supported by a wealth of evidence of integrity. It emerges unscathed from attacks from scientists, politicians, and philosophers.

Your decision to become a Christian joins you to millions of others following a faith based on fact. God has made the human race a fantastic offer. He knows the mess we are in and he has provided a solution. We need to be genuinely sorry for the wrong we have done and ready to turn our back on our old way of life. This is what it means to repent. Next, we must trust that through the death of Jesus, God will forgive us. This is what it means to have faith. When these two things – repentance and faith – happen, God makes his home with us. We are reconciled to him.

These early steps are vitally important. If we don 't really grasp what's going on, or try to skip over the difficult bits, it will actually be harder later on. Think, for example, of young children whose teeth grow crookedly. A brace can correct this fairly effectively. If the crooked teeth are left undisturbed into adulthood the same problem may prove more difficult and take longer to correct. So, let's get our teeth into these two important areas!

Repentance

This means more than just being sorry. Many a criminal has stood in court telling a judge he was sorry. He might simply mean, 'I'm sorry I got caught!' If he commits the same crime a week after being released, it's unlikely anyone will believe that his courtroom apology was sincere. Repentance does mean being sorry – but sorry enough to change. When we repent, we turn our back on going our own way and want to go God's way. It's an absolute about-face, a U-turn, a complete change of direction. International evangelist Dr. Billy Graham puts it like this:

> If your sorrow is because certain consequences have come on your family because of your sin, this is remorse, not true repentance. If on the other hand, you are grieved because you also sinned against God and his holy laws, then you are on the right road.

Many people have fallen at this first hurdle. Some 'prayed to receive Christ' at an evangelistic meeting because they were moved by the emotion of the moment. Some thought they would try Christianity because their friends were involved in it, or it seemed the 'in' thing to do. The trouble is, their Christianity is now gathering dust with the skateboard and the Rubik's cube – once 'in', but now definitely 'out'! All these people wanted Christianity on the cheap – and they got what they paid for: a shoddy, third-rate substitute for the real thing. No wonder it didn't last.

11

Repentance is an essential step in becoming a Christian. It's as if you are saying to God something like this:

Dear God,

I'm genuinely sorry for all the wrong things in my life. Please forgive me. I don't want to live like this anymore. I know that many of the things I say, think and do aren't what they should be. I want to be different. Please help me.

God will certainly hear a prayer like this. Of course, no one is pretending that such a prayer is easy. It's hard enough to say 'sorry', never mind mean it! This kind of prayer costs. It is painful to have to admit we've got something wrong, messed up, failed. Anyone who actually enjoys saying these things must be some kind of masochist. But it's a step that cannot be avoided. Trying to avoid it is like telling the dentist that you want the hole in your tooth filled but you don't want him prodding with any sharp instruments or using his drill. But no drilling, no filling! He can't repair the tooth without getting rid of the decay. If he did attempt it, you'd be back in that dentist's chair within days, the basic problem still unresolved.

Repentance is like the drilling – sometimes painful, but a very necessary first step to getting our lives repaired. Spiritual decay must be dealt with. When it has been dealt with, God's 'filling' has a much greater chance of staying in place.

Faith

Faith is not a blind leap in the dark. Nor is it, as one little boy told his mother, 'believing something you know isn't true!'

Faith is belief followed by action. If we believe that our doctor knows what he is talking about we demonstrate that belief by doing what he says – taking the medicine, changing our diet or following whatever advice he may give us. To say we have faith in him and then tear up the prescription or dump the pills he gives us is hypocrisy.

So when we say we have faith that God will forgive us if we ask him, we must mean that we are convinced he will do so and we will act as if we believe it. That is genuine faith. If I believe that the cup of tea my wife has just brought me will not poison me, I demonstrate that belief by drinking it. If I am still alive several hours later, my belief has been proved correct. I believe that God will forgive me if I ask him. I demonstrate this belief by actually asking him to forgive me. Sometime later (could be weeks, but sometimes it's only seconds!) I discover that I am alive in a new way. My belief was correct.

It is obvious, then, that the genuineness of our faith is determined by whether or not we are prepared to act on it. A prayer we might pray to make our resolve clear would be something like this:

God, I believe you sent Jesus to die for me so that I could be forgiven. Help me to put this belief into practice. Please come into my life and help me to really trust you, not just say I do!

Perhaps you have already prayed prayers similar to those in this chapter. Great! If not, it might be wise to read over the last few pages again, just to be certain you are clear about repentance and faith. If you would find it helpful, talk it through with someone who's been a Christian for a while. The rest of this book will only be of limited help to you until you've got these issues sorted.

Starting out – for groups

Share

How did you become a Christian? Take a few minutes each to share your personal journey to faith.

For discussion / action

Facts and feelings

1 Look back at the cartoon illustration on page 10. Describe to each other your feelings since becoming a Christian. Has it all been good? Or have there been struggles? You might want to make a list of everyone's struggles and doubts on a large sheet of paper.

2 Look up these Bible verses. Members who are happy to read out loud can share them out between them and read them to the group:

John 6:37–40

John 10:27–29

1 John 5:12,13

Romans 8:38,39

2 Timothy 3:16,17

1 Corinthians 15:1–8,20,58

How do these verses make you feel? If the list of struggles you came up with were a list of illnesses, which of these verses would you 'prescribe' to treat which 'illness'?

Next time you feel particularly discouraged, which of these verses do you think would do most to change your feelings?

Repentance

1 Can you remember times when, as a child, you felt guilty about doing something wrong because you were caught? What is the difference between this and repentance?

2 What does 1 John 1:6,7 tell us about the results of repentance?

Faith

1 One definition of 'faith' is 'belief followed by action'. Think of all the people you need to 'have faith in' in daily life – the bus driver, the doctor, etc. What does 'faith' in them mean in action?

The Bible says that God has forgiven our sins and that he loves us. What will faith in this mean in practice in your life?

2 Read Psalm 103:11,12. What has God done with all the wrong things in your past? What does this say about your relationship with God now?

Check out these verses, too:

Romans 6:23

I John 1:9

2 Corinthians 5:17

Ephesians 2:8–10

Prayer

Even after we become Christians, the past can trouble us. Spend a few minutes in quiet thinking over what you have read about God's total love and total forgiveness and give everything in your past – good and bad – to him.

Pray for each other to be able to feel that God loves and forgives you, as well as knowing it for a fact.

2

Joining the family

Yawn … Groan … Oh no! …

For most people, no subject is guaranteed to produced glazed eyes or groans more than going to church!

It's true, the church has a bad press all around. This is not helped by the fact that many church buildings dotted around our communities present a picture of decay and total irrelevance.

Most people expect to visit a church only for 'the three sprinklings' – once with water, once with confetti, once with earth! Anything more than these occasions would seem to be a bit fanatical. Why would anyone in the twenty-first century want to spend time in an old, cold building where people are using eighteenth-century language?

Misunderstandings

Let's clear up a few misunderstandings.

Firstly, the picture of church life we have touched on is true only of some churches. There are thousands of churches in Britain today which are nothing like this. Their worship is lively and the sermons have something to say about life in the third millennium. The services are full of energy and the people are every bit as 'normal' as you or me.

Secondly, despite what you may have seen on TV, clergymen are not all decrepit, eccentric, stupid or from another planet.

Many church leaders are totally in touch with contemporary living, fresh-thinking, imaginative and bright. They are part of the real world and have something positive and dynamic to contribute to their communities.

Thirdly – and this is an area which is desperately in need of being understood – we cannot just go to church, we are the church! The Bible compares being a Christian to being part of a body. When we become Christians we become fingers, elbows or noses! In other words, when God comes into our life, we become attached to other people. The thought of a thumb trying to work while cut off from the rest of the body is laughable. In reality, it just isn't possible. When you come to faith in Christ it is essential that you get thoroughly involved with and connected to a local church. Without the church, you are like a soldier trying to fight a battle without a battalion or a cricketer trying to play the game without a team. Both of these are group activities – and so is the Christian life.

Years ago, a church leader was visiting a man who had become a Christian but who had decided to go it alone. He didn't want to be part of a local church. The leader took a glowing piece of coal from the roaring fire by which they were sitting and placed it in the hearth. As their conversation continued, the once blazing coal began to cool and stopped burning. The point was clearly made. However strong your faith, however much you 'blaze' with joy and life now, without other Christians around you your Christianity is as vulnerable and ineffective as that single piece of coal.

Getting involved

So it's crucial to get involved with a local church. But which one? Well, you may already have one. The chances are that a friend or family member helped you become a Christian. It usually makes sense to go to church with them. But if you haven't yet found a church and are not sure about how to find one, here are a few pointers:

• Don't necessarily go to the nearest church.

• Don't worry too much about which denomination it is.

• Visit several churches before you settle on one.

• Speak to the leaders.

• Make sure the leaders believe the Bible is very important.

• Choose a church where you can sense God's presence in the services.

• You could also try contacting the Evangelical Alliance, who are happy to advise people about good local churches. Visit https://www.eauk.org or phone 020 7520 3830.

Once you are settled in a church, hopefully quite quickly, try to understand the way it works. Who are the leaders? Who should you speak to if you have a problem or a good idea? When does it meet besides Sundays? What does the church expect from you? Sorting out these things early on will save confusion and frustration later.

This would be a good time to raise the question of baptism, which is practiced by many churches. What is done at your church? If you haven't been baptized, there are a number of good reasons why you should be. The Bible says we should be baptized. Jesus himself was baptized. It is a marvelous visual aid of what God has done for us – washing us clean as we have repented and believed. It is also a great opportunity to demonstrate our faith publicly. And, from experience, it's a time when many Christians experience God's touch in a special way. Talk to the leaders about this. (I have written a book on baptism which covers all the reasons as well as the practical and spiritual preparation for taking this step. Being Baptised – the handbook to believer's baptism is also published by Faithbuilders.)

Family

Becoming a Christian means becoming part of the family of God. Once you have settled into your particular part of the family, whether that's in Blackpool, Belfast or Basingstoke, certain responsibilities follow. Being in the family involves certain commitments.

For example, it means we are accountable to others. No family would flourish if its members came and went exactly as they pleased, missed meals at random, paid the bills only when they felt like it, and helped out around the home only when they were in the mood. Healthy family life cannot function well when the members behave like this. Neither can healthy church family life.

Aim to act responsibly from the beginning. Do not miss things without a good reason. When you cannot be there, let someone know, in advance if possible. And if you notice someone is missing, give them a text or phone call, or drop by at their home. Express love and concern. Just think how bothered you would be if a family member failed to come home one night!

And help with the dishes! That is, don't wait around until you are asked to do a job. If you see a need, fill it. When I was growing up, my mother would come in from work and yell to us upstairs where we were playing, 'All hands on deck!' Everyone would leap into action to get a meal on the table. It's amazing what a good meal can be put together in 15 or 30 minutes when everyone joins in. 'All hands on deck!' applies to the church, too. Give out hymn books, put out chairs, give a lift to an elderly person, dig gardens for the disabled, mow lawns – whatever it takes for you to be a productive, contributing member of the church family.

No family is perfect. Even in the happiest homes, there are disagreements and tensions. The church family you join will be no exception. There will be arguments from time to time and people will say hurtful things in the heat of the moment. You may find yourself being criticized or your motives questioned. This is not a cue for you to withdraw into your shell, to stop all constructive contributions, or to retaliate in kind! Neither should it be an excuse to leave the church and go nowhere or to another church. After all, if things get tough at home, you don't go off and find another family. Stick with it; pray for the people involved; act lovingly, and do not talk about it to anyone not involved in leadership.

Talking of leadership, in any family someone has to have the final say in how things are done. Church leaders have a near impossible task and need to be helped, encouraged and followed by the church family. Of course, that doesn't mean that church leaders are to be followed without thought. Good leaders would not want to be. Our general approach must be to get behind the leaders with prayer and active support. This attitude will make it easier for the leadership to guide us – and we usually need a fair bit of this sort of help as new Christians.

When you are at home you can be yourself, take your shoes off, switch on the TV, put your feet up, chill out. In the same way, be yourself in your church family.

Don't put on an act or worry about 'image'. There is absolutely no need to pretend that you are something you aren't. The family will love us – warts and all!

Very many new Christians find this acceptance to be a tremendous relief and even a healing experience. For the first time in their lives, they find that their value is not judged by age, color, qualifications or whatever. They are accepted into a family where these things are not important.

THEY DIDN'T CALL IT "THE FRIENDLY CHURCH" FOR NOTHING

In a church family, you can truly be loved for who you are, not for what you have achieved. Enjoy this new family, particularly if your own family situation is difficult. The single, the divorced, the bereaved, children from broken homes – in a church all can find security and acceptance from a family which will not desert them when the going gets tough.

All this brings us to the greatest privilege of being a member of the church family. We have God as our father. Read the story in the New Testament about the boy who went on a sin binge abroad and wasted his dad's hard-earned cash. You can find it in Luke 15. He lost his friends, his job, and his self-respect, and then had the nerve to return home. His father was no mug. He gave the lad a clip round the ear and sent him off to sleep on a shop doorway. Well, not quite. Perhaps that's what would have happened if you or I had been that father. What actually happened was that he welcomed back his long-lost son, gave him a new set of clothes and threw a party for him!

Every Christian has that kind of father. Before we became Christians, when the last thing we wanted in our lives was God, he loved us. When we make mistakes, get things wrong, fail him and other people – he still loves us. Despite the worst we can do, he waits for us with open arms. You have joined a family where the father is always available, always welcoming, and always wanting to comfort you. There is no 'Do not disturb' notice on his door. He's never missing from the meal table because he's late at the office. There is no problem too big, no sin too great, no failure too awful, no pit too deep, no despair too dark, there is absolutely nothing your father is not capable of dealing with. He loves you.

It is especially important to realize this if you do not have a good 'father model' in your earthly father. Perhaps he died when you were young or deserted your mother. Perhaps he mistreated you or seemed distant and uninterested in your life. If this is the case, do not impose onto God the feelings you associate with that idea of a father. God is all that is best in fatherhood, magnified a thousand times over! In a supernatural way he can become the supportive father you may never have had.

Joining the family- for groups

Share

Before the meeting, one person will need to draw an outline of a church building on a large sheet of paper. On the other side of the paper draw lots of people – pin men will do! Cut the paper into rough jigsaw shapes – enough for every member of the group to have one piece.

When you meet together, each person takes a piece of the jigsaw. On the 'church building' side, write a few words to describe the way you used to see the church before you became a Christian, or how you saw it when you were a child.

Put the jigsaw together and discuss the different responses you've collected.

For discussion/action

Misunderstandings

1 Read 1 Corinthians 12:12–27. Does anything new strike you from these verses? What do they say about your own importance to the church fellowship?

2 What would you find particularly hard if you had to be a Christian on your own, without the support of your church or fellowship group?

Getting involved

1 Read out loud the paragraph about baptism on page 19. If anyone in the group has been baptized as an adult, ask them to talk about what happened.

2 Read these verses:

Matthew 28:18–20

Acts 2:36–39

Acts 8:34–38

Romans 6:1–14

What do these verses say about the purpose of baptism? What is the relationship between baptism and belonging?

3 Read Colossians 2:6–12.

If we sometimes feel discouraged in our Christian lives, or doubt if we really are Christians, how does it help to remember our baptism? What steps can we take to build on the facts to which baptism witnessed? (See particularly verses 6 and 7.)

4 If you are a Christian and have not been baptized, should you consider doing something about it?

Family

1 Think about your own family – past or present. What are the good things about family life? What are some of the struggles? What does this suggest about life together as a church family?

2 No family is perfect. Read together the paragraph on page 20 which starts with that sentence. We may all have struggles about church life, or grumbles about how things are not done as well as we'd like. What's the best, most positive way of coping with these feelings?

3 Read Hebrews 13:17 and the paragraph on page 21 which starts 'Talking of leadership...' How could you make your church leaders' task more joyful and satisfying? If nothing comes to mind, think about some of the difficulties leaders face.

4 If you wanted help servicing your car, would you ask a two-year-old or a car mechanic? Think about the older people in your church fellowship. What particular things do they contribute to its life?

5 Read the paragraphs about God as our Father (page 22). If our biological fathers didn't or don't do a particularly good job, it may

be difficult for us to come to terms with the idea of God as Father. How can we help each other, as brothers and sisters of the same Father, to trust God more?

6 Now each person should take one of the jigsaw pieces again. On the 'people' side, write some of the good things you have discovered about church life, either from your own personal experience or things you've learned from others during this session.

Prayer

Thank God for each other. If anyone has any specific needs or problems they could share with the group, then pray about those issues. Thank God for your church leaders, and for any national or international church leaders that you may have heard about.

3

Doing church

Going to spend time with your new family may seem a huge culture shock to you if you've not been used to attending church. Like all groups, Christians have their own peculiar customs and even language, and they take a bit of getting used to.

There is absolutely no need to dress up to go to church. The days of 'Sunday best' outfits are long since gone. Just wear what you feel most comfortable in. When you arrive, there's often a member of the congregation waiting at the door to welcome people with a shake of the hand. You may find that the welcome person or someone else will be ready to pass you a hymn book, or a Bible, or a notice sheet, or any combination of books and pieces of paper.

In some churches, someone will direct you to an empty seat or pew, but mostly you will be left to find your own way. This can be daunting if the church is a large one and the layout unfamiliar.

Try to arrive in good time. You will find Christians have a habit of filling up the rows of seats from the back, so if you are a little late you will have the added embarrassment of having to sit near the front or even in the front row itself. It's better to arrive with a few minutes to spare than rush in, out of breath and hassled, and unable to concentrate on what's happening while you settle down. Take a few minutes of quiet before the service begins to talk to God, to ask him to forgive you for any area of rebellion against him and ask that he will speak to you during the service. You could also pray specifically for those who are going to be leading and preaching.

When the service is over, stay in your seat a few minutes and pray again. Thank God for any way in which he has spoken to you and ask him to help you act on anything you need to respond to during the coming week. This is such a good opportunity to give God time in your busy week, so don't throw the chance away by rushing into a conversation straight away. Two minutes spent in quiet reflection at this point will make a huge difference to the lasting value of the time you spend in church.

-AND THIS IS A VOUCHER FOR THE CHURCH WEIGHT-LIFTING CLASS...

Before and after the service you may be on the receiving end of very contrasting reactions from those around you. The first scenario is that lots of people speak to you; you may get an invitation to lunch; there may be warm handshakes and even a couple of hugs; someone may say 'God bless you' when you haven't even sneezed! In short, you may find yourself quite overwhelmed with warmth and generosity.

But quite a different scenario is also possible. No one may speak to you at all. There are no invitations for coffee, perhaps just a rather limp handshake. You may find yourself totally underwhelmed by coldness.

Or your experience may be somewhere between the first and the second. Whatever happens, do not be put off. Given time, you will begin to understand your new family and feel comfortable with their behavior.

As for the actual service itself, there may be times when your mind begins to wander. Be reassured that this happens to everyone from time to time. It helps to remember that you are not a spectator but a participant, even though it may look as if you are just sitting there watching what's happening at the front. But actually, those at the front are a bit like prompters in a play. They help us not to forget why we are there – to worship God and listen to him. The congregation are really the actors and God is the audience. Like good actors we want the audience to feel satisfied. As you sit there, ask yourself, 'Is God getting value for money from my worship?'

All this shows that worship is work. Actively try to listen to God all the time – even during the announcements about the outing to Bognor and the evangelistic coffee morning; while you're putting money in the offering; while you're searching for the songs. This all takes your concentration. Come to Sunday worship ready to contribute your best to everything that's going on.

One word of warning while we're on the subject of worship: worship is not primarily about our feelings. Worship is rooted in the will. Unless we learn this lesson quickly we will be at the mercy of our moods. An argument with the kids, a series of late nights, or a tough time at work can cripple our worship. We must make a clear statement in the face of our emotions: 'It is right to worship God. He is Lord, whether I happen to feel like it or not. He is worthy of my worship even when worshipping him is the last thing in the world I want to do. Because it is right, I am going to do it.'

This is more easily said than done, but it becomes easier the more we exercise control over our emotions and resolve to throw ourselves wholeheartedly into worship. Do not be put off by people who claim it is hypocritical to tell God you love him when you do not feel you love anybody! If you have children you will know that they can be stubborn and willfully disobedient. Sometimes they make you very angry. At times like that you may not like them very much at all – but at the same time, you still love them tremendously. This is not hypocrisy. It's just that sometimes the truth is temporarily obscured by emotions. When your anger subsides you feel like loving your children as well as actually loving them.

28

The same thing happens in worship. If we worship despite the way we feel we often find that our feelings come in line with the facts, and we start to feel as if we love God again. If we let our mood dictate what we do, then we end the service feeling as bad as when we started.

The sermon

Sitting still for perhaps 25 minutes – sometimes a lot longer! – and listening to one person speak at you may not seem immediately appealing. It can take some getting used to. There are very few ministers who can hold you spellbound every Sunday with their preaching. In fact, there are quite a few who give their congregations all the thrills of watching paint dry. They couldn't preach their way out of a paper bag!

Being charitable, let's assume that you are listening week by week to an average communicator, someone who does have some gifting in preaching, even if it's not fully developed. Here are some things to remember that will help you get the best out of the sermon.

Remember:

• Nobody gets it right every week. Do not criticize him/her just because they have an 'off' Sunday; pray for your preachers.

• A lot of hard work goes into a sermon. Do not take this for granted. Thank God for such commitment.

• Your own mental, emotional or physical state can affect your ability to appreciate the sermon. Do not automatically blame the speaker if you seem to get nothing from it. It's possible that it might have more to do with your state of health than with the message itself.

• Your attitude is crucial. The atmosphere created by the congregation has a real effect on how the preacher does.

Sometimes the atmosphere presents a thick barrier through which the preacher's words cannot penetrate. Sometimes the atmosphere is so charged with expectancy than even a poor sermon is set alight. So come expectantly and you may be surprised at how much the sermon improves!

Help yourself:

• Bring your Bible. Follow the reading as it's read aloud and look up references given during the sermon.

• Take notes or get a tape of the message to listen to later. You will retain much more this way and so make it easier to act on what you have heard.

• Pray silently during the sermon, asking God to show you what needs to change in your life as a result of what you are hearing.

• If there are things you don't understand, ask someone about them afterward. Don't be too proud to confess your ignorance; if you are, you will likely remain that way!

• If God speaks to you in a clear way during the message, thank the speaker afterward. Not with the 'nice sermon, vicar' kind of comment, but more like, 'I was really helped by what you said about…"

Bread and wine

In some services, bread and wine are shared by the congregation. This can be called Communion, the Lord's Supper or the Eucharist. Depending on the practice of your church, you may have to stay in your seat or go to the front to receive the bread and wine; you may be given your own individual wine glass or be invited to share an ornate goblet or chalice with others; you could be given a thin wafer of something that doesn't look or really taste like bread, or be encouraged to tear off a chunk of a newly-baked crusty cob.

Whatever style your own church uses, the significance is the same. Jesus told Christians to do this. The bread speaks of his body and the wine of his blood. Eating the bread and drinking the wine is a reminder of the life, death, and resurrection of Jesus and is an opportunity to praise him for giving us his new life. Down the centuries God has chosen to use the communion service as a time to be especially close to his people. Many Christians point back to a communion service as a time when they received

31

healing, felt a special sense of God's presence or were given a new direction in their lives. Now that you are a Christian this service is open to you. Approach it with a combination of reverence, anticipation, and joy.

Small groups

Most churches have some kind of small group programme. It could go under a variety of names; home group, housegroup, cell – whatever the description, join one! It may well prove to be the most significant factor in your spiritual growth. In such a group you will learn how to study the Bible, how to pray aloud, how to develop your spiritual gifts (more of that in chapter 5) and hopefully you will also learn how to maintain a sense of humor when someone disagrees with you!

In a small group, you can ask questions, share your own insights, ask people to pray for you and begin to pray for others. In an emergency, the small group leader is only a phone call or a Facebook message away. Be committed to this group of people and they will be committed to you.

Do not underestimate the important role belonging to a small group can play in your life. In larger meetings, it is very easy to remain a spectator, a critic aloof in the stands. A small group helps us to get involved with the action itself, and it is in the middle of the action that our faith is strengthened and refined. Here our weaknesses can be exposed and so corrected, and our misunderstanding about the rules can be put right as they become apparent. Being in a small group can be painful as we expose our inner selves to the gaze of others, but it is a vital part of what God wants to do in us all. Chat with one of the church leaders about joining a group and get started in one as soon as possible.

A natural follow-on from this is to find a helper or mentor who will help you grow in your new faith. This could be someone in the small group who has been a Christian for a while. Ask them if they can spare you some time; an hour a week would be ideal. Use the time to read the Bible and pray together, and to share things that are bothering you which you feel are too trivial or too personal to share in the group. Talk about the successes and failures in your Christian life. Ask their advice. Encourage your mentor to be honest and tell you if there are things he thinks you are doing wrong. Try to accept his/her criticism graciously and give it careful consideration. 'Who does he think he is!' is usually our first response, but loving correction will produce rapid spiritual growth and real Christian maturity.

This kind of help will be especially valuable during your first year as a Christian. It may, of course, continue for much longer and perhaps will develop into a lifelong friendship. For you, the aim is to grow to the point where you feel comfortable in passing on what you've learned by becoming a mentor to someone else.

As you are working through all these suggestions, don't worry if you continually come across bits and pieces of church life that seem very confusing. Different churches have different traditions, types of services, even language. If you find yourself baffled by when to stand, sit or kneel, for example, either ask the person next to you or find someone to quiz after the service. If you find yourself fumbling to find the right place in your Bible for the next reading or don't quite know what to do when the offering plate comes around – just relax! You're among friends. You really will get the hang of things very quickly. It's unlikely that most people will notice your embarrassment and before long you'll be the one able to pass on explanations about the way things are done to someone else.

Doing church – for groups

Share

It's a typical Sunday morning. You've overslept; your husband/wife/dog's in a bad mood. The kids/cats won't stop fighting. You're already 10 minutes late for church – and now the car won't start.

Does this ring any bells? Share with each other what a typical Sunday morning is like for you.

Discussion/action

1 Preparing for church worship is generally thought of in terms of practical things – getting yourself and the family ready in time etc. But what about spiritual preparation? Next Sunday, why not try getting the practical stuff sorted so that you arrive at church with five minutes to spare with the aim of preparing yourself in the ways suggested on page 26. Discuss in the group how you could make this work.

2 How do you feel about the suggestion that in church the congregation are like actors and God is the audience (page 28)? How do you feel about the thought, 'The Lord is pleased with his people' (Psalm 149:4)?

3 Being fed up sometimes is part of everyday life! But we shouldn't let it affect our worship. Read the paragraph on page 28 starting 'One word of warning ...' What things affect your mood?

Read Psalm 42. How does David seem to be feeling? What does he do with his feelings? Do you think God minds what sort of mood we are in when we come to worship? Why/why not? How can you prepare your will and mood for worship?

The sermon

1 What do you remember (if anything!) about the last sermon you heard in church? Share something that God has said to you through a recent sermon.

2 Read through the list of things to do on page 30 to get the best out of the sermon. Are there any more you'd like to add? Any that you'd like to try next Sunday?

Bread and wine

1 Read these verses about the origins of sharing bread and wine: Matthew 26:17–30 and 1 Corinthians 11:23–34.

2 Share your experiences of the communion service, and share ideas for how to get more benefit out of it.

Prayer

Spend a few minutes in quiet thinking about what Jesus has done for us in his death. Thank him for the way he has created a new community of his followers, and for calling us into that community. You may like to share bread and wine together to conclude your session.

4

Enemies

Surely Christians are really nice people who don't have any enemies? Well, it's not quite like that!

When you become a Christian you change sides – from spiritual death to life, from darkness to light. Some of your old allies will notice that you have gone over to the opposition, so look out! Battle is about to commence. It will not be too long before you realize that you are in a war.

Perhaps you feel unprepared for this, but becoming a Christian is more like joining the armed forces than going on a picnic. Every genuine believer experiences opposition, pressure, and attack. There will certainly be days when you wonder why you ever joined up!

It's not all bad news, though. These enemies can be identified, their tactics described, and counter-measures can be put into effect. In this chapter we will look at the 'big three' – what older translations of the Bible call 'the world, the flesh, and the devil'.

The world

This enemy is the worldly non-biblical way of thinking and acting, and it takes many forms. It has one purpose: to make the new Christian want to go back onto the other side by robbing them of the benefits they have received by choosing to follow Christ. Perhaps it takes the form of family members putting pressure on us to give up our new way of life. Many families feel extremely threatened when one of their number 'gets religion'. I have known young people thrown out of their homes or accused of dragging down the family name; husbands who stopped talking to their wives; wives who had to return home to mother –

all because of the new faith. Thankfully, nine times out of ten these separations are temporary, but they are painful. Some have been tempted to give up following Christ for the sake of peace and quiet at home. Make no mistake, family pressure can be intense.

So can pressure from friends. 'Church is OK if you like that sort of thing – but do you have to go so far? You're getting to be a bit of a fanatic!' The pressure can range from gentle teasing to verbal or even physical abuse. You may find yourself socially excluded from groups you were friendly with. You may find people talk about you behind your back, or avoid you altogether. But it's not just in the social sphere that you may experience a decline in popularity. You may even find yourself passed over for promotion in the workplace.

At root, this represents a pressure to conform. Nothing threatens family, friends, and colleagues so much as a change in you which they can't explain. That's why the reaction, 'You'll get over it!' is one of many such encouraging comments you might receive. When the full extent of the radical and permanent change that has taken place in you starts to be appreciated, the opposition may get worse. They want you to conform, while you are beginning to think about things quite differently, come to fresh conclusions, adopt new priorities, alter your behavior. You may find the pressure too much and find yourself drifting back into your old ways. How can you cope with this strong backwards pull?

Here are three strategies that will be of help:

Find a new focus for your security and support

Most people need people to affirm us and confirm that what we are doing is the right thing. In the past, family and friends formed our place of security. Now we want to please God more than anyone else or any group of people. In practice, God delegates some of this responsibility to his people – the church. It's the church that can affirm and support us, even if all our old security systems have failed. It's important that our sense of security moves to rest in God and his people, or we will continue to be heavily influenced by what other people think about us. Ask other Christians to pray for you or even come into tough situations with you. Keep close to God and refuse to be discouraged.

Go on the offensive!

You don't have to allow yourself to absorb all these blows like a spiritual punch bag. Attack! The non-Christian world loves to keep us on the defensive. They know we are in a minority and want to keep us that way. They want us to believe that we are discredited intellectually, outdated morally and declining numerically. Do not believe a word of it! The case for Christianity has never had more compelling academic support; our moral stance is the only clear alternative to the ethical muddles and drifting relativism rampant in our society; and, although in the western world there is a decline in believers, in many other parts of the world there is a significant turning to Christ surpassing anything seen in history. So there is every reason to be confident about your faith. Research the facts so that you can go on the offensive and watch the opposition climb down!

Understand the opposition viewpoint

Recognize how your conversion looks from a non-Christian viewpoint. Imagine how you would feel if someone close to you started to behave strangely. You might genuinely fear for their sanity or believe that they have been brainwashed by a strange cult. Your family and friends care for you a great deal. Be patient with them. Don't be arrogant or patronizing. Once they see that your new faith is genuine and that you aren't going to reject them, things should settle down.

The flesh

Not only will attack come from those around you, but also from inside you, your very humanity or 'flesh'! It's a bit like a self-destruct mechanism. Even though your life has now been given to Jesus Christ, many of the old habits, thought patterns and behavior – 'the old me' – seem to hang around. It can appear like a war is going on inside. One part of you wants to go God 's way, the other part wants to go the familiar old way. The early Christian leader Paul put it like this: 'I don't understand why I act the way I do. I don't do what I know is right. I do the things I hate … The sin that lives in me is what does them' (Romans 7:15,17). From time to time, many of us feel exactly like this.

The way to win the battle with the flesh or self is to starve the old life and feed the new life. Then, obviously, the new life will get stronger while the old weakens. This can only be done a step at a time. It's overwhelming to try to tackle everything that needs changing at the same time. We'll end up frustrated and failing. Instead, we look at every choice as it arises and consciously make the decision that reflects God's way. Each small victory strengthens us and delivers some pretty lethal blows to the old life.

What if we make a wrong decision? Well, it's not the end of the world! We don't have to think, 'I've blown it. Guess I'm just not going to make it as a Christian.' God never gives up on us. There is absolutely no mistake so bad that he cannot forgive and correct if we let him. When the flesh does win, thankfully we have a God who specializes in fresh starts. Have you fallen down? Then put your trust in the God who can pick you up and give you a new beginning. Start again. God will honor your spiritual guts and determination.

If you're looking for some inspiration, let me tell you about Abraham Lincoln. He should have given up long before he became President of the United States. Look at this for a catalog of failures:

1831: Business failed

1832: Election defeat

1833: Another business failure

1834: Minor election victory

1835: Fiancée died

1836: Nervous breakdown

1838: Election defeat

1840: Election defeat

1843: Election defeat

1846: Elected to Congress

1848: Defeated in Congress election

1855: Defeated in Senate election

1856: Defeated in Vice-Presidential election

1858: Defeated in Senate election

1860: Elected President!

Despite all this, he became one of the greatest presidents America has ever had. God is not looking for people who never fail or who never get discouraged. He is looking for people with the humility to admit that they have got it wrong and cannot get it right in their own strength. When they pick themselves up and look to him for his power he gladly supplies it. God is the only one with the power to defeat the flesh – but he needs our cooperation. Paul, who struggled with this issue, raised the question, 'Who will rescue me from this body that is doomed to die?' (Romans 7:24). He was able to answer it for himself in the next thrilling verse: 'Thank God! Jesus Christ will rescue me.'

The devil

There is much confusion about the devil – which, of course, is exactly how he likes it! So perhaps we should start by saying what he is not before we look at what he is and what he does.

He is not:

• a figment of the imagination;

• a slightly irritating bad influence on the world, who would have a pitchfork and a tail if we could see him;

• an all-powerful opposing force to God.

He is a real, evil personality who opposes everything good. His job involves ensuring that the maximum number of people never get round to letting God sort out their lives. Should he fail with some individuals, and they do become Christians, he will be out to rob them of as much joy as possible and minimize their impact on anyone else. The Bible describes him as a cunning master of disguise with all the power of a roaring lion.

Fortunately, he is a roaring lion on a chain! God is the all-powerful keeper of the zoo and will only allow him limited freedom. Not only this but by his Son's death and resurrection God has dealt this enemy of humanity a fatal blow! So he is a mortally wounded lion on a chain! He may not be finished yet, but it is only a matter of time before he is. Christians face a defeated enemy who knows his time is running out. You have nothing to fear.

However, a vicious animal in its death throes can still be very dangerous if we get too close. To treat the devil casually is to invite problems. Watch out for him especially in two areas:

Stubborn habits or obsessions These are not just things like smoking – though if you have a tobacco, drug or alcohol dependency of any kind you need to seek help to deal with it immediately. But, is there something you simply cannot stop doing? You want to stop, now that you are a Christian; you know you should – but you just don't seem able to do anything about it. Perhaps you are a compulsive liar. Perhaps you are addicted to pornography. Are you routinely gambling? Are you consistently unreliable? If there is a compulsion such as this in your life, the devil will love to exploit it. He knows that it's a part of your life over which God has not yet got control, and that makes it an attractive target for him. He will try to get a foothold here and begin to infect everything else from that vantage point.

Involvement in the occult Perhaps before you became a Christian you were involved in some aspect of the occult. You may have just seen it as a bit of harmless fun. You played with a Ouija board, had your tarot cards read, or consulted a fortune teller. Maybe you attempted to contact a dead relative through a medium or attending a seance.

If you feel that any of these activities may have a hold over you in any way, you should deal with it. Very little progress can be made in your spiritual life until the power of evil over your life is broken. Involvement in anything occult is an open invitation for evil forces to take up residence – they need to be made homeless as soon as possible. Here are four steps to giving the devil his eviction orders:

• Stop all occult involvement, even things which may appear trivial such as reading your horoscope.

• Destroy any books or occult paraphernalia.

• Write a list of everything you've done connected with the occult, confess them to God, repent, and ask God to break the devil's influence in your life.

• Share this with your church leaders. They may want to give time to advising and praying with you in a very specific way.

One final word of warning: don't keep on looking for his influence in yourself or others. Don't get absorbed in suspecting demons on every corner. When you discover him at work, do something about it, but otherwise get absorbed in Jesus and focus your attention on him.

Enemies – for groups

Share

In what ways do you think you have changed since deciding to follow Christ – in your thinking, priorities, behavior, attitudes? What pressures have these changes brought?

For discussion/action

The world

1 Read through the three suggestions for ways of coping with the pressures of the world (pages 37,38) and talk over the following questions:

a) Find a new focus for your security and support. Have you found one yet? What do you really trust when the pressure is on? Have you begun to find some security in the church fellowship? Have you found it helpful for other Christians to pray for you?

b) Go on the offensive! Has there been a time recently when you felt 'trapped' by someone criticizing you for your Christian faith? Describe it to the group and discuss tactics for responding to similar attacks in the future.

c) Understand the opposition viewpoint. Imagine that a friend suddenly became a Buddhist. How would you feel? Why might you find it threatening?

The flesh

1 Are you aware of a time recently when evil got the upper hand in your life? Pray together in silence, confessing it to God and asking for his forgiveness.

2 Look at Lincoln's catalog of failures (page 40). Think over your past week. Is there a 'secret diary' of success and failure that you could write? For example:

Monday: Managed not to swear even though I dropped my favorite mug.

Tuesday: Realised I'd gossiped in a very unkind way to Jane about John in the staffroom this lunchtime.

Wednesday: Felt quite unreasonably jealous when Amy told me about her promotion.

Thursday: …

Praise God for the 'successes' you have all experienced this week and ask him for grace to overcome the 'failures.'

The devil

1 'Children, you belong to God, and you have defeated these enemies' writes John (1 John 4:4). God has defeated Satan, so we need not be afraid of him. But he will do his best to keep us locked into old habits. Read John 8:34–36. Is there an unhelpful habit that still has a hold on you? Pray silently, asking God to help you break out of it.

2 Look at Jesus' promise in John 10:10: 'I came so that everyone would have life, and have it fully'. In what ways does this encourage you and give you confidence for the future?

3 Look up Deuteronomy 18:9–13 and Jeremiah 29:11–13. Why do you think God finds people's involvement in the occult so offensive? Why do people turn to the occult?

4 If you have been involved in any occult practices, re-read the section on page 42 and ask the group to support and pray for you as you take the four steps outlined.

Prayer

Pray together for a full release from the grip that evil and fear can still have on our lives.

5

The Holy Spirit

Having begun to see some of the challenges of the Christian life, perhaps you will agree that it's something you can't manage on your own. You need power. Something that's bigger than you. Fortunately, Jesus understands this and has already provided for that need in the tremendous promise he gave for all his followers: 'the Holy Spirit will come upon you and give you power' (Acts 1:8). The Christian's power comes from God himself, in the gift of his powerful Spirit.

Power

Too many Christians try to live the Christian life by huge efforts of will: 'I must stop falling for the same old temptations'; 'I must read my Bible and pray more'; 'I must tell my friends about Jesus', and so on.

Of course, all these are important and we must be committed to working at them. But not on our own! When I take the family on holiday, it is my responsibility to load the car, pack the luggage in carefully, and make sure everyone has their seat belts on. It is not my responsibility to push the car all the way to our destination. Another source of energy – the car engine – has been designed for precisely that job.

Many Christians are worn out and frustrated because they are pushing instead of riding. We begin to ride when we ask God to fill us with his Holy Spirit.

Champions like Tim Henman and other tennis superstars win most of their games because they understand the importance of power when serving! As Christians, we need to grasp the vital message that the Holy Spirit is not primarily given to make us feel good – but to equip us with the power to serve.

You may be the sort of person who is enthusiastic, has lots of clever ideas, plenty of initiative and drive, and full of boundless energy – but these are no substitute for being equipped by the Holy Spirit. God can certainly use our efforts but it is only his power which makes them effective. The Holy Spirit has given gifts to his church to help us support each other and serve the non-Christian community in which we live. You can find some of these gifts listed in 1 Corinthians 12:1–11 and Romans 12:6–8. Notice what a fantastic mix of things are listed here. You can receive anything from the power to heal to the gift of giving your money away! The emphasis is on variety. We do not all have the same gifts but together, using our different gifts, we can encourage each other's skill in serving.

Sometimes it is obvious what our gifts are, but not always. If you are not sure what gifts God has given you, there are ways to find out. Start by asking God to make it clear what gifts he has given you. Ask a friend to pray with you about it. Ask others, particularly those in your home group, to tell you what kinds of gifts they see developing in you. It is often easier for others to see our gifts than for us to see them ourselves.

If you're still in any doubt, then get on and do something! Pitch in and help some of the different organizations linked to your church and see what happens. Does something stir within you when you get involved? How do you react when you go out with the evangelism team giving out invitations to a church event? How do you feel when visiting the lonely or housebound? Or when you cook a meal for the student outreach? Or help out in the creche, youth group or children's church? Go looking for opportunities which might reveal the unique gifting God has given you. As we begin to move out in love to others, all will be revealed.

Beware! There are a couple of dangers which are worth pointing out. Imagine a narrow path, on either side of which are deep ravines. One ravine is called false humility, the other pride. We fall off the track into false humility when we view our gifts as too small and insignificant when we assume that what we have to offer wouldn't be missed if we didn't bother. Perhaps we compare our gifts to those of others and feel jealous. On the other hand, we can fall off the path into pride when we see our gifts as being all-important and indispensable to the church. We feel a dangerous sense of superiority.

Wise Christians stay on the path! Our gifts are different from those of other people but equally important. We need each other's gifts to build an effective church family. Our gifts are not for competition or comparison – but for cooperation! Always remember this, and remind others if you see them forgetting, then perhaps none of us will topple into the ravines!

We've looked at power to serve; now let's consider *power to be different.*

All this talk about gifts for service is good but can be badly spoilt unless we are clear about the second area of the Holy Spirit's activity. He is given to make us more like Jesus. Being filled with God's power and developing it to serve him can happen in a relatively short time frame – but this part of the Holy Spirit's work goes on for a lifetime.

Being like Jesus means growing those qualities that characterized his life. The Bible says 'God's Spirit makes us loving, happy, peaceful, patient, kind, good, faithful, gentle and self-controlled' (Galatians 5:22). These qualities, usually known as 'the fruit of the Holy Spirit' are the kinds of things we should be producing in our lives as we let the Holy Spirit work in us. What a warm, positive set of qualities they are! God's plan is that we should show all these things in our lives more and more as the years go by.

Here are some 'gardening hints' for how to successfully grow bumper crops of the Spirit's fruit.

Remember that fruit takes time to grow. Don't be discouraged by early failures. Say sorry to God and invite the Holy Spirit to help you to be more loving (or happy, peaceful, patient etc) next time. Remember that being a Christian is not a 100-meter sprint –

but more like a marathon. Keep on keeping on!

Apple trees don't produce bananas! A great deal of effort on the part of my human spirit will not produce the same thing as the Holy Spirit. It simply can't. We are looking for the Spirit's fruit, so we need to be cooperating with him, allowing him more and more control of our lives. We can fake it by trying to grow our own fruit for a while, but pretty soon it'll become too difficult to keep up the effort. We're looking for genuine transformation from the inside.

Lazy farmers grow less fruit. There is no getting away from hard work in the fruit-growing business. Farming is hard work, especially preparing neglected soil for planting. Fruit trees must be nurtured and protected from pests of all kinds. It's no easy task. We cannot just sit back and relax, waiting for the Holy Spirit to make us fruitful. We need to commit ourselves to some hard work, consciously working at changing our behavior, our attitude, our speech. A good friend can be a great help here. Ask them to be honest about whether they can detect growth in our lives, or put their finger on where healthy fruit isn't developing.

Pruning is essential. Cutting out the dead wood and excess branches will increase the quality and quantity of fruit. This can be painful but is necessary. How might this work in practice? Well, suppose you ask the Holy Spirit for more of the fruit 'love'. You may be in for a surprise! Instead of the warm, glowing feeling you are hoping to feel, God might send into your life a thoroughly objectionable character who upsets your wife and lies about you behind your back! Just when you feel like throttling him, the Lord reminds you that you asked for the fruit of love to be demonstrated more in your life. This difficult person has given you the opportunity to understand what real love is all about. Hurtful experiences are often God's way of producing a Christ-like character in you.

Being filled with the Spirit

Near the beginning of this chapter, we noted that we receive God's power for living the Christian life when we ask him to fill us with his Holy Spirit. How does this happen?

Firstly we need to understand that God wants to fill us with his Holy Spirit. When John the Baptist was calling people to repentance and dipping them in the river to symbolize their new life, he said, 'I baptize you with water so that you will give up your sins. But someone more powerful is going to come ... He will baptize you with the Holy Spirit and with fire' (Matthew 3:11). Then we read how Jesus promised his disciples as he left them to go into heaven: 'the Holy Spirit will come upon you and give you power. Then you will tell everyone about me' (Acts 1:8). The great evangelist and church planter Paul advised Christians, 'let the Spirit fill your life' (Ephesians 5:18). God longs for us to receive all his marvelous resources.

We need to take a few minutes to ask God, in a simple prayer, to fill us with his Holy Spirit. He will. We may feel a warm glow or a tremendous excitement. A strange language we have never learned may come into our mind. If this happens, just try speaking it out loud. Or we may feel absolutely nothing! However, don't rely on your feelings – but trust in the fact that God wants to fill you with himself. We are all different and God does not impose uniform experiences on us. He respects our personalities.

Many people find that they receive a special touch from God when they are prayed for by others to receive the Spirit. Contact the leaders in your church family and ask for someone to help you pray for this empowering. Or sometimes there's an opportunity to be prayed for in this way during or after church services. Don't be shy!

Expect great things from God. He longs to equip us with his power. Even if you are prayed for and do not sense anything different, do not give up. If you have questions or fears, talk about them with someone you trust. Occasionally God needs to

51

heal a little damage in our lives before he can completely fill us with himself – a bit like mending a hole in a jug before filling it with water. Don't be tempted to think that you are 'too bad' for God to fill you, or that God loves you less than others who seem to enjoy this experience more easily and quickly. Do not let discouragement get in the way of God's work in your life.

Two more things will help us continue towards a mature relationship with a Holy Spirit.

Firstly, do not regard this first experience of the Holy Spirit as a once-for-all-time encounter with him. D. L. Moody, a famous American preacher of the nineteenth century, was once asked if he had been filled with the Spirit. 'Yes', he replied, 'but I leak!' He's not the only one – we all do! We need to keep asking God to fill us with himself. From time to time ask others to pray with you again for a renewed or deeper experience of the Holy Spirit. Being filled with the Spirit is not a destination, but just the departure point. Too many Christians get off the train at the first station when they realize God is doing something in their lives. Stay on the train and you will stay on the rails!

Secondly, do not let any experiences God may give you go to your head! It's all too easy to look down on those who have different experiences to us. But a superior, arrogant attitude will do more than anything else to stop God working in us. If God gives us special experiences we should let them go to our heart, not our head. We do not deserve or earn them – they are gifts. If anything, the greater the blessing, the deeper should be our humility. The more humble we are, the more God can use us.

The Holy Spirit – for groups

Share

How do you react to the word 'power'? How 'powerful' a Christian do you feel you are?

For discussion/ action

Power

'Power' has all sorts of associations for different people. Human power can be used to destroy or to build. The power the Holy Spirit gives is always positive; it gives us the power to serve others and power to become more like Jesus.

1 Look up 1 Corinthians 12:1–11 and Romans 12:6–8. In what areas of your life would you like to be better able to serve God's people?

2 Take off your right shoe and pass it to someone else in the group. Does it fit them? Probably not! Is one size of shoe better than another? How is this a picture of the gifts of the Holy Spirit?

3 Do you know where your gifts lie? Are you aware of any spiritual gifts that God has given you?

4 Read the list of the fruit of the Spirit in Galatians 5:22,23. Which of these do you need to cultivate more in your life? How can you go about that?

5 Pruning is painful but necessary. Read the section on that on page 50. Have you been aware of God using a difficult experience to help you grow more like Christ?

6 Each person should take a sheet of paper and write their own name at the top. Pass them around the group. Under the person's name write down one positive, Christlike quality you have seen in that person. Move the sheets around the group again, and repeat. When everyone has written one thing on every sheet,

return them to the original names – and be encouraged by what you discover about yourselves!

Being filled with the Spirit

1 Look up Acts 1:8; 2:1–4, 40–47; 4:31. What difference did the Holy Spirit make to the disciples? What were they doing after they were filled with him that they were not doing before?

2 Remembering that everyone's experience of the Holy Spirit is different (see page 51), pray for each other to experience the power of the Spirit in a new way. Laying hands on each person as you pray for them can be a helpful symbol of God's loving touch on their lives.

3 Note the two cautions on page 52. Discuss how to guard against them.

Prayer

Spend some time quietly, thinking about your relationship to the Holy Spirit. If you are afraid to ask him to fill you more fully, what is it that makes you afraid? If you want his power, what are your motives? Ask God to help you know how to pray, and tell him that you trust him to give you what's best for you.

6

The Bible

It won't be long before someone will tell you that as a new Christian you must spend time reading that very important book, the Bible.

If you're like most people, you will find this quite a daunting prospect. Perhaps the TV Times is the heaviest reading you do! But do not be put off. Some Sunday papers with their many color supplements contain more words than the New Testament. And, unlike the Sunday papers, the Bible will not be out of date on Monday – and you can actually believe what it says!

Why read the Bible?

There are at least six very good reasons for reading the Bible.

1 *God speaks through it.* No other book in the world is its equal as to how God thinks and what he is saying today. When you became a Christian you met the author – now read more about him in his book!

2 *It tells us how to live.* The Bible gives us guidelines for how to deal with almost every situation – some things to avoid and others to do. It provides a set of values and principles to help us plot our course through the stormy waters of a world where there seems little clear sense of direction.

3 *It answers our questions.* What is God like? Can I be forgiven? Who is really in control of my destiny? Concerns like these are addressed in the pages of the Bible. And there are real stories of real people who encountered God.

4 *It's a spiritual antibiotic.* Taken regularly, the Bible provides protection against the 'disease' which attacks our Christian lives,

namely temptation. Without it, we are very vulnerable to the lies Satan tells us and to the pressure from others to conform to their standards.

5 *It is nourishing food.* Our Christian lives thrive best on a high-Bible diet. Junk food Christians, who exist on occasional binges of celebration meetings and celebrity testimony stories, do not become great men and women of God. The Bible will feed our inner being and bring us assurance and strength in a way nothing else can.

6 *It has the power to change us.* The Bible has the amazing ability to make us different! It can, of course, be read to inform, to educate, or to entertain. It can be appreciated as great literature. But what makes the Bible so different is its enduring power to change generations of Christians as they read it in openness. The Bible shows us what we are like and inspires us to change, to become more like Christ.

Is there a catch? Perhaps you thought there might be!

Difficult, criticized and neglected!

The Bible is not an easy book. Some parts of it are incredibly complex; others are so boring they could be prescribed as a cure for insomnia!

There are several reasons for this. Firstly, the Bible was written way back in history. Even the newest parts are about 2000 years old, and many sections are very much older. It was also written in cultural and political situations that were vastly different from our own. Secondly, the words we read have been translated from another language – generally Greek for the New Testament and Hebrew for the Old Testament. Thirdly, the Bible is more a library than a single book, with a wide range of different types of literature, some of which we are not at all familiar with today, and an equally wide range of subject areas.

There's more bad news to come. The truth is that the Bible is a very criticized book. Quite likely you will find that your view of the Bible has to undergo a radical re-think when you become a

Christian. Perhaps you've understood that the Bible is a history book with a bit of narrow moral teaching thrown in. Almost certainly you have heard that it's a book full of contradictions and impossible miracle stories. Perhaps you've been told that it's a jumble of ancient myths, with a few profound thoughts thrown in. But now that you 're a Christian you're being told to trust it implicitly and follow it without wavering. No wonder you' re confused!

The Bible is a neglected book. You may already have begun to feel that there is a lot of hypocrisy around when it comes to Bible reading. You might discover that Christians who are apparently quite mature hardly ever read this all-important book and seem pretty ignorant of its contents. At a church service the Bible may be read aloud briefly but hardly referred to at all afterward. A preacher you have heard may have used a Bible verse to support an argument they are trying to get across but doesn't seem that bothered to find out what the Bible is really saying. These kinds of experiences can easily give us the impression that the Bible is important in theory – but not in practice!

So how can we deal with these pieces of bad news? The fact that the Bible is not easy should be seen in a positive rather than a negative light. Anything worth having takes time and effort. Unlike the vast majority of books, we will never exhaust all that the Bible has to teach us. Scholars and ordinary Christians alike can spend decades studying it and still have more to discover. The Bible is a book great enough to keep us occupied for our whole life!

There is no need to be too concerned by criticisms of the Bible. The more we read it, the more it convinces us of its truth and integrity. That is not to say that we should not be discerning about reading the Bible, asking questions, and finding out as much as we can about how it was written and what it really means. If you discover things which appear contradictory, do all you can to resolve the issue through study and asking other Christians. As honest critics will admit, after two centuries of facing all kinds of attacks, the Bible has survived intact and well-respected in many scholarly circles. As a report in Time magazine once concluded, 'The miraculous can be demythologized, the marvel explained, but the persistent message of the Bible will not go away.'

Similarly, don't be put off by Christians who don't 'walk the talk' when it comes to Bible reading. Don't condemn them – just determine to be different. Hopefully, you will find other Christians who give a high priority in their lives to the Word of God and aim to live by its principles.

Getting into it

So much for the theory – but how do we begin to get into the Bible in practice?

To start with, it's good to have the right attitude. As we pick it up, we need to have two key thoughts in our minds – reverence and humility. Reverence isn't a word used too much these days. Even the word itself is quite dated. But if we come to the Bible casually, with a 'couldn't-care-less' attitude, its truth will remain hidden from us. The Bible simply does not reveal its marvelous secrets to someone who approaches it like a holiday novel!

And humility. We're very used to skim reading – flicking through the newspaper, magazine, catalog or brochure until we find something that interests us, making split-second assessments of the contents as we go. Quite the opposite happens when we read the Bible: it assesses us! So we need to approach it with a willingness to read it carefully with a view to obeying its teaching.

Once these attitudes are in place we are ready to tackle the practical issues of how to get the most out of the Bible.

Which translation?

There are a large number of different translations of the Bible available today, each in many editions. The choice can be daunting to a new reader. Why so many? Well, some versions are more literal (or word-for-word); others are more freely translated (or sense-for-sense); while yet others are what we call paraphrases – translations which represent interpretations by different individuals or groups.

So how do you know which one to go for? Spend some time looking at some of the range, bearing in mind both what's appropriate for your own general reading level as well as what is most favored by your church.

Here are four I'd recommend that you consider.

• The **New International Version** is a well-respected standard for many churches and sits on the border between word-for-word and sense-for-sense approaches.

• The **New Living Translation** is relatively new and well regarded as a good sense-for-sense translation.

• The **Good News Bible** is another good sense-for-sense translation – older, but still popular.

• The **Contemporary English Version** won an award for its clear English and is a good choice for anyone who's not a great reader.

If you are interested in having a paraphrase alongside a more traditional Bible, the market leader is **The Message**, a very fresh and expressive paraphrase by Eugene H Peterson. Take a look at it in a bookstore before you buy – being very American you may like it or loathe it!

These days it's also possible to buy computer software giving a range of Bible versions, and Bibles for handheld or palmtop computers. Often these have very good search facilities for anyone wanting to do some serious study.

As you grow in your understanding of the Bible you will find it useful to have more than one version so that you can make comparisons. But when you are starting out, there's a lot to be said for sticking to one version and making that the same one that's usually read in your church.

When to read?

The best time to read the Bible will depend on your work schedule and family commitments. It could be first thing in the morning, during your lunch break, when the kids are in bed ... whenever. The important thing is to work out what's best for you and do your best to stick to it, while at the same time not becoming bound by a rigid timetable which becomes a burden. If you do not manage to read the Bible every day, do not worry or feel guilty. However, your Bible reading will be more rewarding if you are disciplined about it. Occasionally it can be really helpful to schedule in a good couple of hours to read the Bible, particularly if you want to get a grasp on a whole book.

Where to start?

Not necessarily at the beginning! Try one of the Gospels, perhaps Mark. This is the shortest account of the life of Jesus. After that, go for one of Paul's letters or another Gospel. In the Old Testament, I'd recommend Psalms and Proverbs before tackling the history books or the prophets. All of the Bible is important – but some bits are particularly helpful.

What if I'm struggling?

Use a good dictionary to look up words you do not understand. A Christian bookshop will be able to recommend a concordance based on the translation you are using. This will list all the words used in the Bible and all the places where they occur. This can be especially useful when you want to find out what the Bible says on a particular topic. Also, if you don't understand why a word is used in a particular verse, it may help to see how it's used in other verses.

There are also commentaries – books written to help explain the meaning either of individual books of the Bible or the whole Bible. These can shed light if the passage you are looking at is particularly obscure or contains some difficult concepts or ideas.

If all else fails, ask your church leader or another mature Christian. If they don't know the answer they will probably know how to find out.

Bible reading notes

More help is available in the form of Bible reading notes, publications which are designed to guide you in your regular reading. Generally, these direct you through short passages each day with notes pinpointing the central meaning and suggesting ways to apply it today. Literally millions of Christians around the world use these helps. The vital thing to remember is that you shouldn't spend more time on the notes than on the actual Bible passage. See page 106 for some recommendations for Bible reading notes.

Reading – and remembering

Some people find it hard to remember what they read. One tip is to vary your approach to reading the Bible. Sometimes read several chapters at one sitting. On other occasions spend all your time meditating on a single verse or phrase. You might want to underline or highlight bits in the Bible that seem particularly relevant to you or make notes in the margin if that helps to fix the truth in your mind. Try to recall the Bible passage you've read some hours afterward and mull it over in your mind. Making an effort to memorize verses always pays off. You could set yourself a target of memorizing one verse a week for the first year of your Christian life. Or you could choose a significant verse from Sunday's sermon and learn that. Once learned, these verses will be there to draw on when sharing your faith with others or resisting temptation.

The Bible – for groups

Share

Talk together about what you most enjoy reading the Bible.

For discussion/action

Why read the Bible?

1 In John 1:1,14, Jesus is described as 'the Word'. Why do you think this is? Have a look at Hebrews 1:1,2 as well.

2 One of the reasons given in this chapter for reading the Bible is that it is a 'spiritual antibiotic' against the 'disease' of temptation. Look up Matthew 4:1–11. How was Jesus able to hold out against temptation?

Getting into it

1 What have you found most difficult about reading the Bible? What have you found most helpful in understanding it?

2 Look through some different translations of the Bible. Share your views about which one you prefer and why. If the one you currently use is difficult to get to grips with, ask the advice of others in the group about alternatives.

3 What times and methods of Bible reading have you found helpful?

4 Look up 2 Timothy 3:16 in all the different versions you have. Discuss the differences and what they contribute to your understanding. If anyone has a study Bible with a note on that verse, read out what it says. If you have any commentaries available, look up this verse and discuss what they have to say.

Prayer

Take time to thank God for giving us the Bible, and that it is a living and life-changing book. Share any particular verse or passages that have meant a lot to you, and thank God for how he has spoken to you through them.

7

Prayer

'Prayer is the most important thing in my life. If I should neglect prayer for a single day, I should lose a great deal of the fire of faith,' said Martin Luther, a great Christian of the sixteenth century.

A lot of people 'say their prayers'. But relatively few people learn to pray! Perhaps before you became a Christian you recited the Lord's Prayer in church, probably without thinking much about it. Almost certainly you have breathed a hurried prayer to God in an emergency. None of this is really prayer. Real prayer involves building a relationship with God.

This relationship-building is not easy. God cannot be touched, seen or heard through our physical senses. Most friendships develop as people talk and do things together and that usually takes time. You cannot invite God back to your place for a coffee. So how do you go about getting to know him?

Talking and listening

Talking to God is not usually too much of a problem. We can tell him our needs, pains, joys, and dreams. We can thank him for his friendship and care, unload our worries and concerns, ask for his help, and let him know how committed we are to making this relationship work. So far, so good.

But what about listening? Friendship is a two-way street and it's pretty frustrating if the traffic is only flowing in one direction.

God wants to talk to us but most of us find it hard to hear him at first. If you were in a nature reserve with the warden he might stop and say, 'Can you hear that woodpecker? You listen

65

carefully and hear the wind, a whole range of bird calls, an airplane, some strange insect sounds – everything, in fact, except the woodpecker! Your ear is not trained to pick out this one sound from among so many others. But the warden's is.

Our 'spiritual ears' pick up all sorts of sounds: our own thoughts and feelings, pressure from others, religious attitudes we have grown up with, temptations from our enemy Satan. Among all the noise is the voice of God. But which sound exactly is him? With time, patience, persistence and guidance from more experienced Christians, we will develop the ability to pick out his voice. We will usually hear him most clearly when we give him our full attention. We may or may not sense that he is present. He might speak to us through the Bible passage we are reading, through a song, through advice and encouragement from someone else. After a while, he will not seem like a stranger at all.

A warning bell!

It is easy, especially for new Christians, to be fooled into thinking that we are hearing God when in fact we are only listening to ourselves. We have two main methods of checking. Firstly, we should remember that God will never tell us anything which goes against what he has already said in the Bible. Secondly, it is very rare to find God saying something which those in spiritual leadership believe to be wrong. It can happen – but if your church leaders do not believe that you have heard God accurately, think long and hard before you go against their advice.

Here is one very practical method of developing your listening relationship with God. You will need a Bible, a notebook, a quiet place and about 20 minutes.

• Settle your mind. Ask God to help you hear him clearly. (1 minute)

• Say sorry to God for failing him; ask his forgiveness. (2 minutes)

• Read a Bible passage slowly, several times. (4 minutes)

• Sit quietly, asking God to help you understand what he is saying in the Bible verses. Write down any verse or idea which strikes you as particularly relevant. (3 minutes)

• Pray, asking God to make you obedient to what he has said. (2 minutes)

• Talk to God in prayer about the things which are bothering you – about yourself, your friends, family, community, and needs in the world. (3 minutes)

• Be quiet. Is there anything else God wants to say? (2 minutes)

• Thank him for his friendship. Tell him how grateful you are for all he has done for you. Sing or read a song of praise to him – remembering that it's your attitude, not your voice that counts! (3 minutes)

• Invite him to spend the rest of the day with you. (1 minute)

Adjust the times shown to fit your own situation. If you find a better method use that instead, or adapt it to suit you, but give it time. You will find that after a few months you can go through this process without the mechanics of the different sections getting in the way.

A common mistake

Many Christians take time to read their Bible and pray, but seem to think that once they have done so they have done all that is required of them until the next: 'time with God'. But no genuine relationship flourishes like this. It would be like trying to develop a friendship with no spontaneity, no dropping in for coffee, no casual telephone call, and acting like strangers if you bumped into each other in the bus queue. How can a friendship grow when it's confined to a few minutes each day as long as something more important doesn't crop up?

Prayer is not to be reserved only for those special times of meeting with God. It should be characteristic of the way we live. An encouraging letter, a beautiful view, a salary rise – thank God for them as they occur. A difficult customer, a worrying interview, a trip to the dentist – tell God your fears during the day. Someone snubs you, someone ridicules you, someone runs into the back of your car – release your anger and hurt to God instead of onto other people! Develop the occasional fleeting 'time out' opportunities during the day, perhaps a few seconds on the train or just before you start the car, to focus on God. Prayer is for all day, every day, not just special times.

Praying with a purpose

All prayer has a purpose. But sometimes we or our church family are faced with situations that require our serious attention in prayer. It could be a recurring problem or a significant opportunity. The church will have ways of responding together, but we also need to make a personal response. Two features of that response could be persistence and fasting.

Be persistent Once a serious issue becomes apparent we may sense that God is urging us to give it special attention in prayer. We can use our normal times of prayer for this and also bring it to mind for prayer during the day, even if just for a few moments. We can ask other Christians we meet to pray about it too and, if we get the opportunity, ask for special prayer at our home group or in church on Sunday.

It is good to set aside a longer time as well to pray just for this issue. This will probably mean sacrificing some leisure time – but an amazing amount of powerful praying can be done by missing an episode of your favorite soap! If we remember to listen to God as well as talk to him, he may also give us guidance on how best to pray. It is thrilling to see the results from this kind of persistent praying.

George Muller was the founder of a number of orphanages in Bristol in the nineteenth century. His whole ministry was built on the principle of persistence in prayer. He wrote:

The great point is to never give up until the answer comes. I have been praying for 52 years, every day, for two men, sons of a friend of my youth. They are not converted yet, but they will be! ... The great fault of the children of God is, they do not continue in prayer ... they do not persevere. If they desire anything for God's glory, they should pray until they get it.

Fast Going without food is another way to focus our minds on a specific prayer topic. The Bible tells of quite a number of occasions when God 's people were encouraged to fast as a sign of how strongly they felt about an issue. Fasting adds a dimension of urgency and power to our praying.

Try it. Go without food for 24 hours and use for prayer the time you would normally spend eating. Simply feeling hungry will also remind you of the topic throughout the day. Do not go around telling everyone you are fasting or putting on a pious face. It is important, however, that you explain to your husband, wife or family well in advance that you will not be joining them for certain meals, and why. Drink plenty of liquids and you will be fine. If you are pregnant or have specific health problems it will be a good idea to chat first to your doctor.

Praying together

Praying is like music. Instruments played on their own are good, but there is a depth and richness of sound when a number play together. Praying with others will deeply enrich your prayer life. The Bible promises God's special presence when groups meet for prayer, and it records some pretty spectacular answers to prayer. Have a look at the story of Peter's miraculous escape from prison as an example of the power of group prayer (Acts 12:5–17).

So get involved in praying with others. If your church has a prayer meeting, go along. If it does not, there will be other opportunities in small groups. No one finds it easy to pray out loud at first, so here are some practical steps that will help you get and give the most to your group time of prayer.

• If you are really nervous, write out a brief prayer in advance, then read it out during the prayer time. Or you could read out a meaningful hymn or verse from the Bible.

• Do not pray long prayers; they can really interrupt the flow of a meeting. A good general rule is to pray long in private and short in public!

• Use everyday language. Be real. Do not put on a pretend 'spiritual' voice. Just speak as if you were talking to a wise father.

• Pray more than once if there is time, but do not make it difficult for shy people to get a prayer in.

• One prayer/ one subject is a good guideline. Some people reel off every problem they can think off in a two-minute 'world tour'. When they say 'amen' there's often nothing left for anyone else to pray about!

• Encourage others who are praying by saying 'amen' out loud at the end of their prayers. Listen carefully to what they say so that your 'Amen' is sincere!

• Try not to 'preach' at people during your prayer or pass on juicy bits of gossip under the guise of prayer. Both of these come into the category of 'propaganda' rather than prayer.

• Pray positively. Avoid using prayer as an occasion for a good moan. Your positive prayer could encourage others and set a really good tone for the whole prayer time.

In many churches, prayer meetings have quite a bad reputation. Even in home groups which have super Bible studies and lively social occasions, the prayer time can be about as exciting as watching paint dry! Your contribution, along the lines suggested, can make all the difference.

Prayer partners/prayer triplets

Another great way to strengthen your prayer life is to find one or two other people to pray with on a regular basis. Make sure you do not idle the time away with coffee and chat. The regular commitment will inject discipline into your prayer life and encourage your faith as you see God answering prayer. When one partner is down, the other can encourage; when one has had an answer to prayer, the joy is shared. Having one or two others to be accountable to can help you stay focused in your Christian life.

Prayer – for groups

Share

Talk together about both the difficulties and the help you experience in praying.

For discussion/action

Fewer questions have been provided for this session so that a longer time can be spent praying. So decide within the group whether that will take the whole of the session or part; and, if part, when the praying will happen.

You could adopt the pattern of prayer set out on pages 66, 67, allowing a little more time for each step if you are doing this as a group rather than as an individual activity. A suggestion for the Bible passage to study during this prayer time would be Luke 11:5–13. Rather than write down your ideas, you could discuss them together.

For further discussion

1. Think about yourselves involved in everyday activities – shopping, changing the baby's nappy, chatting to a friend on your mobile, driving to the office. How can you stay as aware of God's presence at these times as when you are praying alone and undisturbed?

2 Read Isaiah 58:1–10. Fasting is not a matter of twisting God's arm to get him to answer our prayers. What does this passage tell us about fasting? How does it relate to the way we live our lives?

3 Read the section on praying together on pages 69, 70. How could you contribute more to the prayer life of your church?

8

Telling others and looking outwards

Evangelism is a topic we all seem to approach from quite different perspectives. Some people just can't keep quiet about becoming a Christian! Every conversation, whether it starts off about football or the weather, ends up with them enthusing about their faith. If this is you, fantastic!

On the other hand, some people never seem to feel anything else but very embarrassed about becoming a Christian! Asking them about it reduces them to red-faced stuttering. If that's you, then this chapter will help you start telling others positively about the Jesus you've met and developing a concern for the wider world.

Why bother?

Why is it so important to pass on our faith to others? There are four main reasons.

1 *Gratitude and sharing.* Suppose you have just made an amazing discovery – a medicine which cures heart disease within weeks and with no nasty side effects. You were critically ill, but taking the medicine has brought you a complete recovery. Several of your friends have tried it and it has had spectacular results. To keep the news to yourself while thousands continued to die of heart disease would be uncaring and callous beyond belief. God has forgiven the evil in our lives, wiped away our guilt, made us part of a new family, given us access to supernatural joy and peace, offered us power for living, guaranteed us eternal life … gratitude compels us to let others in on the secret!

73

2 *Obedience.* Sharing our faith is not an optional extra, as if only those going for some kind of deluxe version of Christianity need bother about it. When we joined God's army we recognized a new commanding officer. Our lives are now under his authority. His wishes are clear: 'Go to the people of all nations and make them my disciples ... teach them to do everything I have told you' (Matthew 28:19).

3 *God works through people.* How did you become a Christian? Probably through a friend or relative. How are others going to hear the good news if not through you?

4 *Need for rescue.* Men and women who reject Jesus are doomed to meaninglessness now and separation from God eternally. If we do not throw them a lifebelt we will be abandoning a drowning generation as they sink under the waves of hopelessness.

Know your defenses

Have you noticed how sportsmen and women are wearing ever more impressive high-tech protective gear these days? Cricketers, for example, are wearing more padding and helmets with face guards. As Christians, we often feel like we are facing high-speed spin bowling wearing only our underwear! Can we cope with the questions about our faith that people are going to throw at us?

There are two key ways to improve our defenses.

1 *Anticipate the questions* Remember the questions you had before you became a Christian. Things like, 'How can Christianity be true if the church is full of hypocrites?' or 'Is Jesus any more than just a good man?' or 'Hasn't science disproved the existence of God anyway?' There are a limited number of questions which crop up.

Find a Christian book with some good answers to these questions. [Modesty isn't going to prevent me mentioning my own book *It Makes Sense* here – details at the back!] With a little bit of preparation you will feel more comfortable answering these questions.

Sometimes we get asked questions to which we just don't know the answers. Be honest and admit you do not know! No one knows the answer to everything – and those who ask questions do understand that.

2 *Know your faith.* You may not be an expert on science, other faiths, philosophy ... any number of topics. But you can determine to be an expert on the Christian faith. You will quite quickly be able to have a better understanding of the Bible than pretty much any non-Christian – and that will put you at a real advantage.

Go on the attack!

Being well protected as a cricketer isn't much use if you're just going to stand on the edge of the pitch. The aim is to score runs. Similarly, in evangelism, we not only have to be able to answer people's questions but also to be ready to initiate discussion ourselves.

If, for example, someone asks us to justify our faith in the light of all the suffering in the world, we can give a reasonable answer. When we have done this we can go on the offensive and ask the questioner how they would explain the world's suffering.

Do not hesitate to turn an awkward question back to the person who asked it. Jesus himself used this method to great effect.

Look for openings to talk about your faith. Don't do this in a 'pious' or unnatural way – just talk as if you were chatting about a good film or something you saw on the TV news. As long as you do not preach to people or talk down to them, they will be interested.

Ask other people about themselves. Very few people can resist talking about themselves, especially with someone who is genuinely interested. The information you gather will help grow the relationship, and people will be more open to listening to you.

Live the life

We may have our lines of defense and attack clearly thought out, but to make them effective we need to give some attention to how our lives match what we say. Nothing undermines what we say about Jesus more than saying one thing and living another. Here are eight tips that will help bring the two into line.

1 *Be relaxed.* Don't become a nervous wreck by working flat out to be perfect. You are not perfect – but God will use you anyway. Besides, you will communicate your anxiety, not your faith, if you get too uptight about witnessing.

2 *Keep your cool.* Try not to flap, even when teased or provoked about your faith. Laughter is great at relieving tension. Walk away rather than lose your temper.

3 *Get involved.* Be a good family member and a committed employee. Do your fair share of work at home and in the workplace.

4 *Watch your language.* Non-Christians expect Christians to give up swearing – so don't confuse them!

5 *Be balanced.* Religion should not be your only topic of conversation or church your only leisure activity. You need a good bit of 'secular' fiber in the diet for healthy living!

6 *Be normal.* It's not likely Jesus has turned you into a cross between Mother Teresa and the Archangel Gabriel. So there's no need to act as if you come from another planet or walk around with a holy smirk on your face. Fanatics and frauds will put people off very quickly.

7 *Be a friend.* If you have not been a Christian very long you probably still have a lot of non-Christian friends and family members. These are precisely the people with whom you should be sharing your faith. Take time to keep these relationships strong. It would be wrong to neglect them anyway. But your friends will be particularly unimpressed if you dump them because of your Christianity! Avoid isolating yourself in a totally Christian world. Because of the pressure of time, you will need to limit the number of jobs you do in the church if you are to develop friendships effectively.

8 *Train.* In one sense, evangelism is the most natural thing in the world – just telling other people about something good that has happened to us. In practice, most of us would benefit from a little training. Sometimes a church offers training or may be willing to bring in an outside evangelistic agency to run a training course.

Power and evangelism

God has changed our lives by his power. The same power is available to change others. You can have complete confidence in this. It may seem hard to believe, but your most unpleasant relative or most obnoxious colleague can be made different by God's power. The same power which has been affecting people's lives down the centuries has not lost its potency today.

Looking outwards

In earlier chapters, we have looked at my prayer life, my future, my church, my spiritual gifts and so on. All essential stuff. We must get these things right if we are to grow as Christians. But can you see how we can become very inward-looking? My this and my that... I have known Christians who assess every service, every ministry, every gift by what they can get out of it. We are in danger of breeding a self-centered, self-serving generation of Christians!

We need to look outward in order to have a balanced Christian life. Jesus himself is our great example in this. He took time to meet his own needs – food, sleep, relationship with the Father – but was still known supremely as someone who put a high priority on other people and their needs. He focused his life on God first and then looked outward to the needy world.

We are vulnerable to being inward-looking simply because we live in a society which is dominated by self-interest. So many things about our culture have 'me' at the center. We are all infected. Religious selfishness is no answer to worldly selfishness. Selflessness is our goal. Ask God to help you keep looking outwards.

Mission

Billions of people around the world do not know about Jesus. Millions do not have the freedom to speak about him publicly for fear of arrest or harassment. Hundreds of thousands do not have any part of the Bible in their own language. Look over the walls of your own church, beyond your own community, past the frontiers of your own country and into this vastly needy world. We have a bewildering array of Bible versions, books, websites, apps, CDs, DVDs, magazines and ministries to help us. But many people have never seen a Bible, let alone owned one. Many countries have tiny percentages of Christians, and missionary activity is almost non-existent. Some countries discriminate against Christians and respond to the gospel with repression or imprisonment. We need to open our eyes to these realities.

Prayer

Find out about other countries. What are their specific needs? How many of the population are Christians? What Christian agencies work there? A mine of information is the book *Operation World* by Patrick Johnstone (OM Publishing) or the website www.operationworld.org.uk, which gives relevant facts and figures. You could adopt a missionary, perhaps with others in your prayer group, and commit yourself to regular prayer for them.

Giving

Many Christians spend a good deal more on feeding their pets than on giving to missions in other parts of the world! How do you do? And your church? Consider adopting a mission organization or a particular project and give a regular amount in addition to your regular giving. Or what about sending letters, emails, text messages or the occasional parcel of goodies to encourage a missionary working in a tough place? Approach a mission organization if you want to be linked with someone in this way and they will be able to advise you on what will be appreciated and appropriate.

Community

When thinking of mission, don't ignore the community on your doorstep! As new Christians, the temptation is to dump all our old non-Christian friends, develop a new set of friendships and throw ourselves wholeheartedly into church life. This can lead to us ignoring the very people we are supposed to be reaching with the news about Jesus! Withdrawing from all 'non-spiritual' activities in the community leads to the church becoming a ghetto, increasingly absorbed in its own activities and progressively isolated from the community it is supposed to serve. What began in the early days of the church as a powerful, loving and relevant community has deteriorated in twenty-first century Britain to become a sterile, introverted religious clique! Many people in your area probably don't even know where your church meets, let alone what it teaches or who its leaders are.

Here are three basic steps you can take to make sure you don't get detached from local community life.

1 *Re-discover your neighborhood.* Walk along the streets near your home and take a good look around! What are the strengths and weaknesses of the area? What kind of people live behind those net curtains? How would Jesus respond to what you see? Find out all you can about the area. The local library and the local government offices are good places to start.

2 *Re-order your priorities.* Simple to say – tough to do! You need to ensure that time is given to activities outside your own fellowship. Perhaps you could manage one night a week in a non-church-based pursuit. If you can find something that also involves your partner or children then that also expands the time you can spend with the family. It may mean that you have to turn down a church job to preserve this community involvement.

3 *Re-evaluate your programme.* Just because the church has a football team you don't have to join it! You could join another local club. If you're into aerobics or line dancing or mud wrestling or knitting, think twice about starting a group at church. Why not look for one locally? Support the school band, go along to the local fete, join the operatic society, sign up for the cricket team.

There are many opportunities in our own localities to exercise a major influence for good. School governing bodies need committed representation. Town or parish councils need people. Residents' associations need committee members. Local charities need volunteers.

Don't forget the influence of the media. Is your local or community newspaper looking for a district news reporter or a sports columnist? What about local radio?

These ideas represent just a small fraction of the opportunities we have to serve our communities.

Issues

Our society has many problems which have been around for a long time, but these days the internet brings them into our homes with an immediacy that is hard to avoid. Racism, AIDS, domestic violence, alcoholism, drug abuse, abortion, paedophilia – these are just a few of the issues that regularly feature in the news headlines.

As Christians it would be wrong to bury our heads, ostrich-like, in the sand and hope these problems go away. We cannot indulge in the luxury of the 'I'm alright, never mind about the rest of you' version of Christianity which is content to let the world go to hell while we enjoy the benefits of our personal salvation. Our God grieves over these issues – and so they should be of real concern to us.

Give money, sign petitions, write letters and enthuse others! Each act, however small, combines with the efforts of other people to have a potentially major impact. Government policies, broadcasting schedules, the attitudes of multi-national companies – all of these have been changed by protest, sometimes by just a handful of polite but persistent people!

Telling others and looking outwards – for groups

Share

Role-play a discussion between one or two Christians and one or two people who have never heard of Christianity before. The task of the Christians is to explain what their faith is all about. Let the conversation improvise for about five minutes. Then become your 'real' selves again. What did those playing the Christians find most difficult about talking with those playing non-Christians? What was hardest to explain? How convincing were they? How did everyone feel as they were talking/listening?

For discussion/action

How important do you think it is to share our faith with others, and why?

Know your defenses

1 What questions did you ask about Christianity before you became a Christian? How would you answer them now?

2 Read John 4:1–26. How did Jesus put some of these principles into practice?

Power and evangelism

What do you find most difficult about sharing your faith? Talk with others in the group about any fears or misgivings you have.

Mission

What missionaries are supported by your church? Could you offer help? Could you commit yourself to write on a regular basis? Or contribute to their support? Or organize an information board about them?

Community

Find a time when your group could go on a prayer walk around your neighborhood. In twos and threes walk around, praying for those areas and for the people who live in the houses you pass, who work in the offices or factories, the children who go to the schools, and so on.

Afterward, discuss anything that struck you particularly in terms of the needs of the area. Is there anything practical that you or your group or your church could do to help?

Issues

What social problems are a particular feature of your locality? How could the church be better involved?

Prayer

Pray about the issues that are in your hearts. Ask God for wisdom to know how much you should take on and for his guidance in knowing how to be most effective in what you do.

9

Lifestyle issues

When we first become Christians, many of us make the mistake of thinking God is only interested in the 'religious' part of our lives. We think he wants us to pray and go to church, but we assume he has no interest in our normal day-to-day activities. Nothing could be further from the truth!

When we become Christians we become God's special children and, as our loving parent, God is vitally concerned about every aspect of our lives. He has things to say about marriage, singleness, sex, money, work, and leisure. You name it and he wants to be involved in it!

And he is uniquely qualified to do so. He made us, so he knows what makes us function properly. Think of one of those flat- pack wardrobes. They're hard enough to put together at the best of times – but imagine putting one together without the instruction sheet and wearing a blindfold! Our lives can only be lived properly if we follow the Maker's instructions. And if we're new Christians and unsure of the instructions, we shall need some help to discover them and start putting the principles into practice.

Before we look at some of the principles, we need to be sure about one thing. Doing what God says in these areas is not what makes him love us. We cannot earn his love, recognition or approval. He gives us these as free gifts. We obey his rules, not as a way of collecting ticks in boxes but because we love him and want to please him. When we try to obey God without love for him, we find we are performing a joyless duty. This is both frustrating and discouraging as we realize that we can never live up to his standards, no matter how hard we try. It is then only a short step to giving up completely on any attempt to do what God's standards demand. But if we love God we will want to do what he says. And, because we know that his love does not depend on how well we succeed, we can relax when we fail and be encouraged to try again.

The principles

How do we know how God wants us to behave? There are three ways of checking, which act as a map, a compass, and a guide, all showing us the right way to go. If all three point in the same direction, then we can be pretty certain of being on the right track.

The map

The Bible is the Christian's map. The first and most crucial step is to know what it says. It deals with some aspects of lifestyle clearly, but others are not addressed directly. For instance, we will not find references to cruises, high-performance cars or abortion. But we will find principles relating to our use of time and money and to the value of life, along with some detailed application of those principles to situations that were faced by first-century Christians. Jesus' teaching and the letters in the New Testament set these out clearly.

The compass

When we have discovered what the Bible says on a subject relating to the way we live, we must adjust our behavior to fit the Bible, not the other way around. We are the compass and need to decide how to bring ourselves into line with the map. This will mean thinking about how to apply the Bible's teaching in our situation. As well as thinking carefully about it, we need to pray about it, asking God what he wants us to do. This is especially important where the Bible seems to be silent or unclear about an issue. One thing to remember here is that God will never guide us to do something which goes against what he has already said in the Bible.

The guide

When we have come to a decision about how to act in a particular situation, we need to check it out with a guide – someone who knows the territory pretty well. What do mature Christians say? Ask the leaders in your local church how they deal with the issue in their own lives. How do they come to believe what is the right course of action? Do they think the decision you have come to is the right one? What advice would they give you?

Another way to find out what reliable Christians believe is to read a good book on the subject. Your minister or the manager of your local Christian bookshop should be able to help you find one.

The specifics

So much for the general principles. Now for some specifics. When we become Christians some of the ways we think and act need to change. We will look at two big issues in personal lifestyle and see how our new faith affects them.

Sex

The Bible's teaching on sex can come as a bit of a shock, especially if you didn't know much about Christianity until recently. Put plainly it's this: sexual intercourse is fantastic. In fact, it was God 's idea in the first place. Sex is never described as dirty or sinful in the Bible. But there are unmistakable rules. Two of the most basic rules are that sex is only to be expressed within marriage, and that homosexual activity is wrong.

This goes completely against society's current thinking. It could hardly be more counter-cultural. Our society preaches 'safe sex', encourages girls in their young teens to go on the pill, and idolizes media superstars who change their sexual partners as often as they change their cars. All this makes it pretty tough for the new Christian. Hardly anyone seems to believe what the Bible says about sex anymore. Well, there are two things you can take comfort from.

Firstly, *just because something is popular doesn't make it right.* God's standards are pretty unpopular in the twenty-first century – but that's no indication of them being wrong.

Secondly, *God's standards work.* Casual one-night-stand sex becomes deeply unfulfilling. Committed sex with a lifelong partner is one of life's most rewarding experiences. Comparing the two is like putting a fast food burger alongside a gourmet meal. God's standards are also much healthier for society. The epidemics of STDs (sexually transmitted diseases) and AIDS would be almost non-existent if people followed God's plan of chastity before marriage and faithfulness within marriage. Many countries trying to control the spread of AIDS by making free condoms available are losing the battle. The radical, biblical alternative is by far the most effective solution.

So much for the facts. But knowing them is no good unless we go on to change our lifestyle. If you need to change your behavior in this whole area of sex, then remember some practical things:

It will not be easy Old habits die hard, so you may find yourself under great sexual temptation. Prepare for this in prayer, and ask others to pray, too. Avoid putting yourself in situations which encourage you to give in to pressure. Plan how to fill your time with alternative and productive activity.

Be bold The longer you take to implement your new lifestyle, the harder it will be. Do not be conned into the 'I'll wait until I'm a little stronger in the faith' syndrome. That is about as logical as waiting until you feel a bit better before starting to take the medicine! Tough action, taken soon, will be a significant factor in your growth as a Christian.

Be humble That is, do not become a self-righteous prig! Just because you have decided to bring your sex life into line you should not look down on others who have not. Your non-Christian friends will not take kindly to a holier-than-thou attitude.

Be persistent We live in a society which encourages promiscuity. Sex is used to sell everything from cars to ice cream, and sexual indulgence is constantly encouraged. In this environment – even having discovered God's standards – you may slip back into sexual sin. God still loves you. Say sorry to him and pray for strength. Be determined to live a life which pleases him. With his help, this is a battle you can win.

Be sensitive Your boyfriend or girlfriend may not share your new faith. You will need to explain carefully why you have decided to change your sexual behavior. He or she may feel hurt, thinking that you are rejecting them, or even that you have found someone else.

Please note: if the situation is further complicated because this is a particularly long-standing relationship or you share a home or if you have children then you will probably need some help in planning a way ahead. There is no off-the-shelf solution here to resolve how you can honor both your commitment to your partner and to God. Don't alienate your partner but seek appropriate advice from Christian leaders.

Money

This is probably the other main preoccupation of men and women at the beginning of the twenty-first century. We cannot survive without it and the goods and services it buys. The problem is that it seems to dominate our thinking and can warp our attitudes and change our behavior just as effectively as a. drug. The more we have of it, the more we want. None of us is immune to the pressure of living in a world where our creed is greed and our god is gold. So what is God's attitude?

Despite what many people think, the Bible does not say that money is the root of all evil, but that it is the love of money which is so corrupting (see 1 Timothy 6:10). When we love money it starts to own us, rather than the other way round. These principles will help us make it our servant rather than our master.

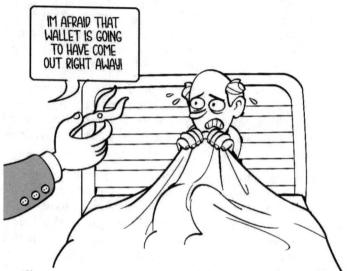

All our money is God's When Jesus becomes our Lord he becomes the owner of every aspect of our lives, including our money. The right question to ask is not, 'How should I spend my money?' but 'What would Jesus like me to do with his money?'

Give generously Some of God's money ought to be given for use in God's work. The Old Testament suggests that we should give ten percent of our income to this (a tithe). Ten percent is still a useful guideline today but is a very difficult target for some to achieve. You may need to take a few months sorting out and rearranging your finances before you can get to this point. If you are more highly paid you should find the ten percent target easier to achieve and can consider going beyond. Plan to give that money when you get your pay, rather than leaving it to see how much is left at the end of the month.

Avoid waste Because our money is God's and can accomplish so much, we should try not to waste it. Be careful about hasty purchases and impulse buying. It is not a bargain if you don't need it or is so cheap that it will break within three days! Examine your motives. Some brands are bought to impress. Are you buying to impress anyone or keep up with the neighbors?

Plan borrowing carefully Debt has become a national problem. Only use credit cards if you are certain you can settle them promptly. Be wary of long-term repayments because your situation may change unexpectedly. Aim to live within your means. If you feel you need advice or are anxious that you are getting into financial deep water, look for a friendly accountant in the church to talk to, or a recommendation for someone with expertise in this area. The longer you leave it, the harder it will be to sort out.

Warning! The map – or Bible – tells us that stealing is wrong. That includes crying to cheat the tax man or submitting inflated expense claims. Watch out for the dangers of gambling. What starts out as a couple of lottery tickets can end in a full-scale addiction.

Sex and money are not, of course, the only issues with which the Bible can help us. The Bible is surprisingly full of God's views on almost all the areas which affect the way we live – everything from bringing up children to old age, from friendship to behavior in the workplace. Find out what God has to say and begin to put it into practice.

Lifestyle issues – for groups

Share

Watch an episode of Eastenders or your favorite soap on catch-up. Talk together about how the decisions, actions, and attitudes of the characters might have been different had they been Christians.

For discussion/action

The principles

Many things about which we need to make decisions are not specifically mentioned in the Bible: whether to smoke, whether to go on strike, which bank to use, which charities to support, whether social drinking is OK, how much of your budget to spend on NETFLIX, and so on. If the Bible doesn't say anything directly about these things, how can you make your decisions?

The specifics

1 'Right is right, even if everyone is against it; and wrong is wrong, even if everyone is for it.' What do you think of this quote? Who seems to have the loudest voice in society today when it comes to saying what is right and wrong about sex? Why do you think that is?

2 What would Jesus like you to do with his money? Think about how you spend your money. Do you know what you spend it on? Is there anything you need to change?

3 Giving away ten percent of our income is known as tithing (see page 90). Think about how much you currently give to God's work. If there is a gap, is it practical for you to close that gap?

4 'If you ill-treat the poor, you insult your Creator' says Proverbs 14:31. Most of us waste a great deal and yet are very acquisitive.

Is there any way in which these habits can be said to be ill-treating the poor?

Prayer

Share with the group any decisions you have made recently about changing your lifestyle. Pray for each other as you put them into practice.

10

Guidance

Human ingenuity has succeeded in guiding space rockets as far as Mars, guiding planes safely through every kind of foul weather, and guiding deadly missiles accurately to small targets hundreds of miles away. But we seem incapable of coming up with a foolproof guidance system that works for the average human being! Despite all the sophistication of our twenty-first century societies, as both groups and individuals, we are often totally unclear as to the way ahead. We are baffled by some of the choices and decisions we have to make. Sometimes it seems we are going around in circles – just rather more quickly than we used to!

Every day thousands of people scan their horoscope in the hope of some clue to guide their lives. Some consult astrologers or mediums. If there was a book entitled How to Make all the Right Decisions about your Future – in Three Easy Steps it would sell millions!

Guided – not programmed

'Will that course really help my career?' 'Should I apply for that job?' 'Is this the best time to move house?' 'Is this the right marriage partner for me?' 'What can I do to get out of this mess?'

None of these questions has a slick, easy answer. But when we are Christians we can say that the essential question is, 'How can I discover what God wants me to do with my life?' As we search for an answer to this question we need to bear in mind that we are sons and daughters of a wonderful Father God. His desire is not to treat us like robots, programmed for every trivial task. We have genuine freedom. Some of us are far too intense about the issue of guidance when God wants us to relax and realize that if we stay close to him we need not worry too much over most of our decisions. When we are walking with him he can guide us almost without our knowing!

There is one piece of really good news to start with: God wants to guide us! As Psalm 32:8 says, 'I will point out the road that you should follow. I will be your teacher and watch over you.' His long term goal is for us to become like Christ. He's not in the business of concealing things from us or making life difficult as we work towards that goal. As a caring father, he wants his children to have the best. So we can approach him for help with complete confidence.

In a world where people, in general, want to please themselves, Christians want to please someone else – God! There are two main reasons.

Firstly, God made us and so knows how we function best. Thousands of products carry this piece of advice: 'For best results, follow the maker's instructions'. Stamped indelibly yet invisibly on every human being are the same words! Christians look to God because he's the one with the greatest knowledge about how we 'tick' as individuals.

Secondly, only God knows the future. Absolutely everything is in his plan and control. So who better to help us prepare for it?

But, how does God guide? What does he use to direct us? Here are eight aspects of his 'guidance system'.

1 *The Bible.* Through the regular reading of the Bible we come to see what kind of people God wants us to be. The Bible sets general boundaries around the areas we have to decide about. For instance, if you are a man looking for direction about getting married, the Bible gives advice about the qualities you should be looking for in a wife in terms of character. It will also indicate that she should be a Christian and that you should see a relationship with her as being permanent. The Bible will not give you her address and telephone number!

Sometimes a verse of the Bible leaps off the page at us and seems to indicate a specific course of action. This can be a real help ... but be careful! Make sure God is giving the same message through some of his other methods of guidance as well.

2 *Prayer.* God can use our prayers to speak to us about his purpose for us, especially if we develop the art of listening! Over a period of time, as we listen to God, a sense of peace or 'rightness' can come over us about the decision we have to make. An inner conviction often develops that this course of action is the one we should take. The Bible puts it like this: 'Don't worry about anything, but pray about everything. With thankful hearts offer up your prayers and requests to God. Then, because you belong to Christ Jesus, God will bless you with the peace that no one can completely understand. And this peace will control the way you think and feel' (Philippians 4:6,7).

3 *Circumstances.* God is often working for our good without us knowing it. Opportunities arise, coincidences occur, and tragedy may strike. All these things form part of our lives. God can take all these events and use them to help us discern his will. The Old Testament tells the story of Esther, an ordinary person who became a queen. Her uncle helped her to see that she had not risen to prominence by chance; God could use that circumstance to enable Esther to rescue her people from death. 'It could be that you were made queen for a time like this!' he said (Esther 4:14).

4 *Common sense.* The trouble with common sense is that it is not very common! God made us and he knows our gifts, skills, and limitations. If you are five feet two inches tall he is probably not calling you to be a basketball player. If you can't hold a tune you are unlikely to become a concert pianist. Occasionally, God overrules major obstacles like this, but more often than not they are a pretty reliable guide to what our future is likely to be.

5 *Leaders.* The Bible puts us in a special relationship with the leaders in the church. 'Obey your leaders and do what they say. They are watching over you,' says Paul (Hebrews 13:17). Seek their advice. Ask for their help. Do not assume you can get by without consulting mature Christians now and again. At the very least they can listen carefully and pray sympathetically. At best you could find yourself on the receiving end of some wise insights that had never occurred to you! Only pride prevents us from getting someone else's input for our situation. Do not jeopardize your future by missing out on this vital method of guidance. 'Fools think they know what is best, but a sensible person listens to advice,' says Proverbs 12:15.

6 *The supernatural.* God sometimes guides by speaking directly to us. An idea comes into our head right out of the blue; a mental picture fills our thoughts, or words of instruction come into our mind. When people pray for us they may be given something from God to pass on to us. People have occasionally been given visions or God has used a dream to speak to them. Even angels get sent with messages from time to time.

Christians often seem to take one or two extreme positions about this form of guidance. Some will not make any decision without some kind of special revelation from God; others think that this sort of guidance hardly ever happens today. Be balanced! God can and does guide in these ways today. Be open to him doing so. However, do not be obsessed with this one method of guidance to the exclusion of others.

7 *A sign.* Sometimes people ask God to give them a sign to confirm what he wants. The classic example in the Bible is that of Gideon. One evening he put a fleece on the ground and asked God for the fleece to be wet with dew and the ground dry when he got up the next morning if God really wanted him to take a particular course of action. When God did this, Gideon asked him if he could do the trick the other way round for the following day! God did. After this convincing display, Gideon was sure what he had to do!

From time to time Christians have asked God to confirm his will by giving them a miraculous sign like this. Many of them have been deeply disappointed! This form of guidance needs to be handled with real care. We cannot treat God as a kind of celestial magician who can be asked to perform magic acts as a guarantee of his will. Taken to its logical conclusion this would remove the need for faith altogether. It has to be said that God does sometimes honor requests for this kind of sign but we need to be careful about putting God to the test. It is only likely to be a useful method of guidance on special occasions; we should not try it every time we want to discern God's will.

8 *Duty.* Not too popular, this – but very important. It is no good claiming that God wants you to phone up the boss to say you are sick so that you can take the day off to evangelize your friends! That is not what God wants; he sees that you have a duty to your employer. There is no need to pray about whether to pass on a bit of gossip you picked up at church. Don't do it; you have a duty to others in the body of Christ. Some things are wrong and some are right. However much we pray for guidance in these matters, the facts will not change! Sometimes guidance is as simple as just doing what you know to be right.

Of course, not all these forms of guidance will be appropriate on each occasion. Usually, we can act if a number of these things point in the same direction. When they seem to point in conflicting directions, wait ... and keep on seeking. If all eight point clearly in the same direction God has got something pretty amazing up his sleeve for you!

The principles

Now that we have established the methods God uses we can go on to look at three key principles by which we can discover his will in practice.

1 *Ask* 'Pretty obvious,' everyone thinks. But is it? How many times is God the last person we consult about a decision instead of the first? God does not ram his guidance down our throats, he waits to be asked.

That is why the Bible is constantly encouraging us to ask. Jesus says 'Ask, and you will receive' (Matthew 7:7). James says, 'If any of you need wisdom, you should ask God, and it will be given to you' James 1:5). The key is to involve God early in our decision making – before we have time to come to any conclusions which are hard to change.

2 *Obedience* God will not guide us unless we are willing to do what he says. Too many people use God as one source of guidance among many. If they want to take his guidance, they might – as long as it fits in with everything else. Or they treat God like a doctor who has diagnosed something they did not like the sound of ... they go somewhere else for a second opinion. With God, there is no second opinion! We must be ready to do what he says. We are soldiers reporting to a commanding officer, not members of a debating society. Jesus himself was bound by this principle. Faced with the awesome prospect of the cross, he recoiled from its horrors. Despite this, he was clear about where his priority lay: 'do what you want, and not what I want,' he said to his Father God (Luke 22:42). It is people with this attitude who are given God 's guidance.

3 *Action* Do not sit around in your Christian life waiting for some flash of lightning to guide you. Act on what is right and, as you do, be open to God speaking to you. Abraham was told by God to leave his home town, but not where to go! It was only as he traveled that God told him. Just as it is much easier to steer a car that is moving, so it is much easier for God to guide us when we are in action for him.

Guidance for groups

Share

Is there any aspect of your life which feels as if it's drifting or going around in circles at the moment?

For discussion/action

1 Paul writes, 'We know that God is always at work for the good of everyone who loves him. They are the ones God has chosen for his purpose …' (Romans 8:28). What is God's ultimate aim for us in life? How are we able to achieve this? To help as you discuss this, check out Romans 8:9, Ephesians 1:17 and Ephesians 3:16–19.

2 Some Christians think that God has a 'best plan' for their lives and if they miss it they will end up with a 'second best' life. How do you respond to this idea?

3 How do you feel about your relationship with God? Do you think of him more as a friend or foreman? How will each of those two ways of thinking affect the way you expect him to guide you?

4 Read John 15:15,16 and then 15:13. In saying that we are not his servants but his friends, Jesus is also implying that we are working alongside him in his Father's business. What does this suggest to you about the scope Jesus gives us for making our own decisions?

5 There's no such thing as a Christian professional burglar. Why not? Can there be such things as Christian accountants? Christian politicians? Christian soldiers? Christian teachers? Why or why not? What principles do you have to take into account before deciding whether or not God is guiding you into a particular job?

The principles

1 Many Christians talk about 'hearing God speak' to them. From what you have read in this chapter, how would you say God does speak to us? In what ways have you known him speak to you? How did you know it was God and not your own imagination?

2 Is there anything you think God is asking you to do or to stop doing? How are you going to check out what he is saying? If he is speaking to you, what should you do about it?

Prayer

Pray together about any decisions members of the group may be facing. Close by saying these verses together as a prayer of trust: 'We depend on you, Lord, to help and protect us. You make our hearts glad because we trust you, the only God. Be kind and bless us! We depend on you' (Psalm 33:20–22).

It's the last session!

If you 've found the group helpful, share your experiences and feelings. Now's a good time to discuss whether you are going to continue meeting. If so, what will be the group's main purpose? What are the practical arrangements? If not, what are you going to do next to help you continue to grow as a Christian and mature as a follower of Jesus?

And finally ...

As you finish this book or complete your sessions as a small group, you may feel you are getting to grips with the basic ingredients of Christian living. Hopefully, the chapters have given you enough information to lay firm foundations for the future. But you have hardly started building yet – and the construction work will take you the rest of your life!

Here are some suggestions to consider as you look ahead and try to build on the foundations you've laid so far.

Go for steady progress

This book gives lots of ideas to think about and plenty of things to be doing in order to grow as a Christian. You could be excused for thinking that you need 30 hours in every day and 10 days in every week! Relax! Take it a bit at a time. Steady progress is better than three months of frantic activity followed by a state of nervous exhaustion. It's not a sin to take time out to go to the cinema or have a meal out with friends. God is with us in our leisure and can use us just as effectively there as in our church-based activities.

Try not to get too intense about the Christian life. Develop a good sense of humor and do not take yourself too seriously. Laugh regularly with – but not at! – other people. I'm sure there are times God finds us amusing so the sooner we get in on the joke and learn to laugh at ourselves the better! The ability to laugh at ourselves is a key factor in moving towards maturity. It can protect us from pride, deliver us from depression, keep us from criticism and save us from stress. As a general rule, most Christians should take God more seriously and themselves less seriously.

Keep going!

The devil uses a variety of things to get people to give up their Christian faith: pressure from friends or family, failure, a crisis, other attractions or some sin we refuse to put right. It could even be something trivial like the minister forgetting to visit you in the hospital or not being asked to sing in the music group or not getting asked to be a home group leader. He will use any ploy to try to separate you from God and his people. Be aware of this and don't let anything knock you off course in your faith. Determine right now, with God's help, to let nothing get between you and God or between you and his people. You are in a committed relationship with God, one even more permanent than the marriage bond promises to be 'till death us do part'. In our relationship with God, even death does not bring separation, only more joy!

Don't be discouraged

You may feel fed up with how slow your progress seems to be in the Christian life. Perhaps you feel disillusioned because none of your friends or family show any interest in Jesus. It can be pretty discouraging if your church seems stuck in a rut or your home group is as enthusiastic as a turkey at Christmastime.

But don't let discouragement rob you of joy, stop you witnessing, make you less committed to the church or push you into reverse in your spiritual growth. Many of the great achievements in God's kingdom took years to accomplish, triumphing over incredible odds and only finally succeeding after countless set-backs and disappointments.

Keep on keeping on. Persistence is crucial. God will honor your faithfulness and you will have the joy of his 'well done' on your life. You may also find yourself accomplishing something very significant for God.

More to come

On your trip from London to Glasgow, you have just reached Watford. On your journey down to the south of France, you are only now leaving Dover. In other words, you are hardly out of nappies ... you are just getting started on your Christian life! There is so much more to come – more about the Bible, more about the church, more about ourselves. Above all, there is more about God. There will always be more of God to discover and experience. Go for it!

Other books from Stephen Gaukroger, also available from Faithbuilders Christian Publishing

Being Baptised An essential and accessible book for anyone curious about or considering believer's baptism as a part of their journey of growing faith.

It Makes Sense Best-selling humorous and compelling look at the reasons it makes sense to be a Christian. Covers science, suffering, other faiths, and many other issues.

Suggested Bible Reading Notes

Various Daily Readings for Advent from Faithbuilders

Various Daily Readings for Lent from Faithbuilders

Encounter with God from Scripture Union

Everyday with Jesus from CWR

Our Daily Bread from Our Daily Bread Ministries

CPSIA information can be obtained
at www.ICGtesting.com
Printed in the USA
BVHW041712081019
560540BV00012B/89/P

9 781532 696008